The Pembroke Welsh

Corgi

An Owner's Guide To

A HAPPY HEALTHY PET

Howell Book House

Howell Book House
A Simon & Schuster Macmillan Company
1633 Broadway
New York, NY 10019

MACMILLAN is a registered trademark of Macmillan, Inc.

Library of Congress Cataloging-in-Publication Data

Harper, Deborah S.
    The Pembroke Welsh corgi/ [Deborah S. Harper].
      p. cm. (An Owner's guide to a happy healthy pet)
    Includes bibliographical references.
    ISBN 0-87605-214-6
    1. Pembroke Welsh corgi. I. Title. II. Series.
    SF429.P33 H375 1998
    636.737—ddc21
98-37226
CIP

ISBN: 0-87605-214-6

Manufactured in the United States of America
10 9 8 7 6 5 4 3 2 1

Series Director: Amanda Pisani
Assistant Series Director: Jennifer Liberts
Book Design: Michele Laseau
Cover Design: Iris Jeromnimon
Illustration: Patricia Douglas
Photography:
    Front cover: Jane Rainsford
    Front cover inset: Pets by Paulette
    Back cover: Mary-Elizabeth Simpson
    Janet Bodin: 34
    Linda L. Canfield: 82
    Deborah S. Harper: i, 5, 9, 19, 32
    Normajean: 33, 35, 41, 42, 44
    Howell Book House: 23, 25
    Cheryl Primeau: 36, 51, 57, 66, 68, 91
    Bob Schwartz: 9, 18, 22, 24, 28, 38–39, 40
    Mary-Elizabeth Simpson: 7, 11, 29, 33, 34, 48, 54, 61, 64, 71, 75, 85
    Jean Wentworth: 2–3, 12, 16, 20
    Ellan Young: 30, 45, 63
Production Team: Carrie Allen, Toi Davis, Stephanie Mohler, Terri Sheehan

Contents

Welcome
to the
World

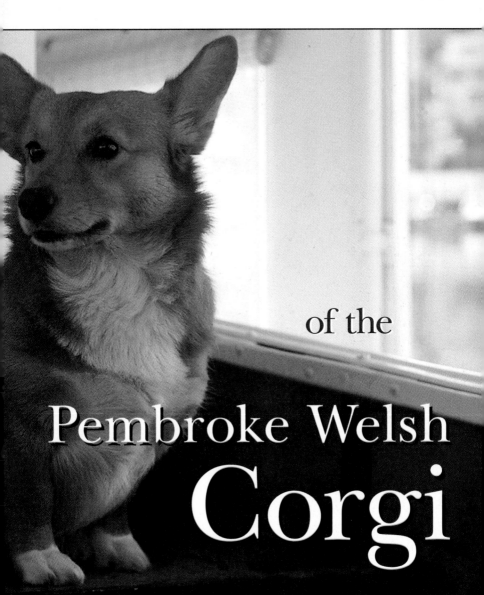

of the

Pembroke Welsh
Corgi

External Features of the Pembroke Welsh Corgi

chapter 1

What Is a Pembroke Welsh Corgi?

The Pembroke Welsh Corgi is a hardy little dog with a long body and very short legs. His foxy head with pricked ears and bright eyes denotes alertness and keen intelligence. The medium length, weatherproof coat sports a face framing ruff of longer hair around the neck. The style of his tailless rear is enhanced with plush furnishings.

Pembrokes are surprisingly heavy for their size. They have sturdy bones and strong muscles, yet they can move with astonishing speed and great agility. They are often referred to as "a big dog in a small package." These attributes came in handy on the Welsh farmland where the breed was developed primarily to herd cattle. His job

description has changed in modern times, however. He now applies his considerable talents to being a top-notch companion animal.

The Pembroke Welsh Corgi is included in the American Kennel Club (AKC)'s Herding Group, along with much larger breeds such as the Collie and German Shepherd Dog. Alongside this company, he competes very successfully at the AKC's conformation shows and other events.

The Breed Standard

WHAT IS A BREED STANDARD?

Every recognized breed of dogs has a written description known as a standard. This very important document states exactly how an ideal example of the breed should appear. The overall structure of the dog and every part of the body is spelled out in minute detail. The desirable way for the dog to trot across the ground is an essential element of the standard. Even the temperament and basic personality are included. If the standard is well written, its reader should be able to call up a mental image of the breed.

The special characteristics of the Pembroke Welsh Corgi are clearly described in the standard. A good way to learn the basics is to start with this blueprint of the breed. The standard is repeatedly studied by serious exhibitors and dedicated breeders who strive for top-quality Corgis. It also includes directives to judges called upon to officiate at dog shows. Below are excerpts from the official Standard of the Pembroke Welsh Corgi, which was approved by the AKC in January of 1993. Quotes from the actual document are

WHAT IS A BREED STANDARD?

A breed standard—a detailed description of an individual breed—is meant to portray the ideal specimen of that breed. This includes ideal structure, temperament, gait, type—all aspects of the dog. Because the standard describes on ideal specimen, it isn't based on any particular dog. It is a concept against which judges compare actual dogs and breeders strive to produce dogs. At a dog show, the dog that wins is the one that comes closest, in the judge's opinion, to the standard for its breed. Breed standards are written by the breed parent clubs, the national organizations formed to oversee the well-being of the breed. They are voted on and approved by the members of the parent clubs.

printed in italics, and comments and explanations appear in regular type. As the entire standard is quite lengthy, the most pertinent points have been selected for review here. A complete version can be found in the AKC's *Complete Dog Book,* published by Howell Book House, or can be acquired by contacting the American Kennel Club at 5580 Centerview Drive, Raleigh, NC 27690-0643.

GENERAL APPEARANCE

Low-set, strong, sturdily built and active, giving an impression of substance and stamina in a small space. Should not be so low and heavy-boned as to appear coarse or overdone, nor so light-boned as to appear racy. Outlook bold, but kindly. Expression intelligent and interested. Never shy nor vicious.

Correct type, including general balance and outline, attractiveness of headpiece, intelligent outlook and correct temperament is of primary importance. Movement is especially important, particularly when viewed from the side. A dog with a smooth and free gait has to be reasonably sound and must be highly regarded. A minor fault must never take precedence over the above desired qualities.

The first sentence reflects the initial impression of the breed. As a herding dog, the Corgi needs to be fit in mind and body and ready to take on the task at hand with enthusiasm and endurance. His wise approach to life coupled with a distinct sense of humor are endearing characteristics. The dogs (males) should be masculine without being coarse, and the bitches (females) should be feminine without lacking substance. A Corgi with proper skeletal proportions and firm muscles will achieve the breed's purposeful ground-covering gait. The total picture of any individual dog is the relationship of all these factors to each other. No one attribute is more important than another.

A Corgi should be moderately long and low.

SIZE, PROPORTION AND SUBSTANCE

Height (from ground to the highest point on withers) should be 10 to 12 inches.

Weight is in proportion to size, not exceeding 30 pounds for dogs and 28 pounds for bitches. In show condition, the preferred medium-sized dog of correct bone and substance will weigh approximately 27 pounds, with bitches approximately 25 pounds. Obviously oversized specimens and diminutive toylike individuals must be severely penalized.

Proportions *Moderately long and low. The distance from the withers to the base of the tail should be approximately 40 percent greater that the distance from the withers to the ground.*

The overall balance and outline, so important to correct breed type, are determined by the proportions of the height, length, thickness of bone and body weight. For example, a heavy-boned dog with a short body will look clunky but may actually weigh the same as a long dog with spindly legs. Neither is correct. Starving or stuffing a dog so that it complies with weight stipulations does not improve overall balance if the height-to-length ratio is off. However, any dog is always more attractive and healthy with tight muscles and firm flesh. Substance, as stated in the beginning, should neither be overdone nor racy.

A Corgi that is a good length but too low to the ground because of overly short legs might tire while working out in the pasture (and his original purpose is still pertinent to the breed standard). A dog with a square outline simply lacks breed type. It is the specific "moderately long and low" ratio that is an essential characteristic of the Pembroke Welsh Corgi.

HEAD

The head should be foxy in shape and appearance.

Expression *Intelligent and interested, but not sly.*

Skull *Should be fairly wide and flat between the ears. Moderate amount of stop. Very slight rounding of the cheek,* *not filled in below the eyes, as foreface should be nicely chiseled to give a somewhat tapered muzzle. Distance from occiput to center of stop to be greater than the distance from the stop to nose tip, the proportion being five parts of total distance for the skull and three parts for the foreface.*

Although the Pembroke Corgi has a "foxy" shaped head, he should not have the narrow, pointed nose and squinty eyes of a fox. The line of the skull, when viewed from the side, should be parallel to the line of the muzzle. A steep skull line or rounding between the ears is faulty. The correct amount of stop (the space between the eyes where the skull meets the muzzle) is important. Too abrupt a change along with a heavy brow gives a blocky look. Too flat a stop leaves a plain appearance. The standard is very specific about the proportions of skull to foreface. The correct five-to-three ratio is essential for a good Pembroke head.

Part of the Corgi's "foxy" look derives from the size and shape of its ears.

Part of the foxy look comes from the erect, medium-sized ears, which taper to a slightly rounded point. The ears are placed on the top of the skull and slant outward slightly. Corgis move their ears constantly and most expressively. They usually are carried pointing back as the dog trots along. Large, rounded "bat" ears are atypical, as are short, pointed "kitten" ears.

The eyes, including the rims, are oval and medium in size and set somewhat obliquely. They can be various shades of brown in harmony with the coat. A dark brown eye, but not truly black, is preferred. Light eyes are undesirable, as they give a hard, staring expression. The eye rims should be black to match the lips and the nose. Sometimes a fine row of black hairs outlines the rims like mascara.

Another important breed characteristic is that a *line drawn from the nose tip through the eyes to the ear tips, and across, should form an approximate equilateral triangle.* This triangle solidifies the correct proportions of the head and placement of the eyes and ears.

The final stipulation about the head is that the teeth should meet in a scissors bite, where the inner side of the upper incisors touch the outer side of the lower incisors. A level bite, where the edges of the incisors just touch, is acceptable, but any other arrangement is a Very Serious Fault.

NECK, TOPLINE AND BODY

Neck *Fairly long. Of sufficient length to provide over-all balance of the dog. Slightly arched, clean and blending well into the shoulders. A very short neck giving a stuffy appearance, and a long, thin or ewe neck are faulty.*

Topline *Firm and level, neither riding up to nor falling away at the croup.*

The topline is the part of the back from the withers (highest point of shoulder) to the base of the tail. In the Pembroke Corgi this line should be level with the ground. A slight dip is permissible where the heavy neck coat meets the shorter body coat, but the back should not arch up over the loin nor drop to a low tailset. The topline should not ride up in the rear. A well-constructed Pembroke will have a level topline even when he is trotting across the ground.

Body *Rib cage should be well sprung, slightly egg-shaped and moderately long. Deep chest, well let down between the forelegs.*

The deep chest and fairly long rib cage contribute to the impression that this is actually a medium-sized dog with short legs. The chest drops well below the point of elbow but should not reach to the pastern (wrist). The correct egg shape allows for proper shoulder placement. A capacious rib cage provides ample room for the heart and lungs.

A large portion of the Corgi's length comes from the front of the chest to the end of the rib cage. The loin, which is unsupported by anything but the spine, should be relatively short, as the dog must be able to twist and turn instantly in his occupational chores.

Short legs support the Corgi's relatively long body.

One of the most distinguishing features of the Pembroke Welsh Corgi is his lack of a tail, and thereby hangs . . . a tale! In the early days of the breed, many Pembrokes were born tailless or with short stumps. This in no way hampered their activities. While taillessness is a strong genetic factor, it is not due to a defective gene. Over the course of time, breeders selected their stock for other features to improve the breed, and the gene for a "natural dock" submerged in the gene pool. Most of the puppies born today have long tails, which according to the standard are docked as short as possible without being indented. Up to 2 inches in length is allowable if it doesn't spoil the contour of the topline. This is done a few days after birth.

In recent years several countries, including Britain, have enacted a docking ban on all breeds. Breeders

*Most Corgi pup-
pies are born with
a long tail that is
usually docked
shortly after they
are born.*

have been working with bloodlines that still carry the gene for a natural bobtail and have produced some fine Corgis without sacrificing other desirable breed qualities. In the United States, docking is still allowed. Nonetheless, a few bobtails appear in litters from time to time.

FOREQUARTERS

Legs *Short, forearms turned slightly inward, with the distance between the wrists less than between the shoulder joints, so that the front does not appear absolutely straight. Ample bone carried right down into the feet. Pasterns firm and nearly straight when viewed from the side.*

It is important that the front legs of the Pembroke Welsh Corgi not be perfectly straight from the elbows to the ground. Because of the shortness of leg and deep chest, the forearms (the bone between the wrist and the elbow) have a slight curve so that the wrists are closer together than the elbows. However, this curve should not be exaggerated, and the pasterns and feet should be parallel and face forward. Too much of a curve and/or feet that face east and west are unfortunately common faults that indicate a weakness in the running gear.

The shoulder blades are long and slope back along the top of the rib cage. The upper arms, which connect the shoulder blades to the forearms, should be nearly equal in length to the shoulder blades. The angle between the blade and the upper arm at the joint is approximately 90 degrees. If the length of the upper arm is correct and the angle is right, the point of elbow should fall in a line perpendicular to the ground directly under the withers. A short upper arm places the point of elbow under the neck and restricts the forward motion of the front leg. Short upper arms are a common fault.

The ideal Pembroke Corgi foot is oval with the two center toes slightly in advance of the outer toes. Strong, well-padded feet are a necessity, as they carry the entire weight of the dog and must be tough to cope with rough terrain. To avoid mishap in the field, dewclaws (extra toes on the inside of the legs) are usually removed at the time the tail is docked. The nails must be kept short to maintain the tightness of the foot.

HINDQUARTERS

Ample bone, strong and flexible, moderately angulated at stifle and hock. Exaggerated angulation is as faulty as too little. Thighs should be well-muscled. Hocks short, parallel, and when viewed from the side are perpendicular to the ground.

The stifle is the knee joint, which connects the thigh bone to the second thigh bone (the upper leg bone). The word "hock" is actually used for two things—both the heel joint and the bone that follows down to the foot. The angles mentioned in the standard refer to the joints between the bones. The legs from the hock joint to the foot are "short and parallel."

In order for the Corgi to move efficiently, the hindquarters must be comparable to the forequarters. The rear produces the driving action, and the front legs reach forward. If the angles between the main bones of these two assemblies are widely different, an imbalance occurs. In other words, if the angle of the shoulder blade to upper arm is greater than 90°, while the thigh to second thigh angle is close to 90°, things do not go smoothly. The hind legs have a greater range of flexibility and drive than the front legs, and the imbalance in angulation results in inefficient action.

Another problem to watch out for is overly long hocks—"hock" this time referring to the back leg bones. Long hocks are a common cause of a topline that rides up behind. Lack of angulation at the stifle will do the same thing. With a wider than 90° angle at the stifle, the hind legs have restricted motion and result in a short stride with poor rear thrust. Good movement is a result of proper conformation.

COAT

Medium length; short, thick, weather resistant undercoat with coarser, longer outercoat. Over-all length varies, with slightly thicker and longer ruff around the neck, chest and on the shoulders. The body coat lies flat. Hair is slightly longer on back of forelegs and underparts and somewhat fuller and longer on rear of hindquarters. The coat is preferably straight, but some waviness is permitted.

One of the grandest attributes of the Pembroke Welsh Corgi is the coat—it sheds dirt, doesn't tangle and protects the dog from temperature extremes. It's also a reasonable length, easy to care for and rain resistant. The thick undercoat is not noticeable, but adds to the luxurious feel of the coat. The variation in length provides the attractive full ruff and fancy pants as well as the charming "fairy saddle" clearly visible at the withers and over the shoulders.

The downside is that the Corgi's is a shedding coat, and the dog can be expected to experience a seasonal lack of furnishings. Also, Corgi genes frequently produce a cute but faulty type of coat called fluffy—a Very Serious Fault according to the standard. (The Pembroke Welsh Corgi standard has no disqualifications—only Very Serious Faults.)

The term "fluffy" or "fluffies" refers to a *coat of extreme length with exaggerated feathering on ears, chest, legs and feet, underparts and hindquarters.* The fluffy coat is soft, silky and without the usual hard outer guard hairs to repel burrs and snags. Such a coat is a hazard for a working dog, hence the serious fault status. A fluffy must not be shown. Trimming the coat does not make it any more acceptable. In fact, the standard is emphatic that NO trimming except for the whiskers and hair on the feet is permitted.

COLOR

The outer coat is to be of self colors in red, sable, fawn, black and tan with or without white markings. White is acceptable on legs, chest, neck (either in part or as a collar), muzzle, underparts and as a narrow blaze on head.

Pembroke Welsh Corgis appear in a wide variety of colors and shades, and usually are bedecked with flashy areas of white. Reds range from a dark "foxy" color to a pale fawn. Sables are red dogs with black tips to the guard hairs, giving the coat a shading of black. Some sables are heavily shaded, and some have only a smattering of black, mostly on the shoulders, skull and tailset. Often sables show a distinctive cap-like marking over the eyes lending to them an elfish expression.

Tricolors come in two basic versions—the "red headed tri" and the "black headed tri." The black on a "red headed tri" can be just a saddle across the back or spread over most of the body. The margins between black and red have a tweedy appearance. The adult head is mostly red with just a touch of black here and there.

The "black headed tri" has a distinct pattern. The skull is black, there is a black stripe on the bridge of the muzzle, the ear tips are black, a black crescent sweeps

THE AMERICAN KENNEL CLUB

Familiarly referred to as "the AKC," the American Kennel Club is a nonprofit organization devoted to the advancement of purebred dogs. The AKC maintains a registry of recognized breeds and adopts and enforces rules for dog events including shows, obedience trials, field trials, hunting tests, lure coursing, herding, earthdog trials, agility and the Canine Good Citizen program. It is a club of clubs, established in 1884 and composed, today, of over 500 autonomous dog clubs throughout the United States. Each club is represented by a delegate; the delegates make up the legislative body of the AKC, voting on rules and electing directors. The American Kennel Club maintains the Stud Book, the record of every dog ever registered with the AKC, and publishes a variety of materials on purebred dogs, including a monthly magazine, books and numerous educational pamphlets. For more information, contact the AKC at the address listed in Chapter 13, "Resources," and look for the names of their publications in Chapter 12, "Recommended Reading."

back on the cheeks and there are noticeable brown dots over the eyes. Overall, this is a much blacker dog. If there were no white markings, the legs would be brown, and there would even be black dots on top of the toes and brown under the tail. (The black and tan pattern is perfectly illustrated by the Doberman Pinscher.) In Corgis, white usually masks the total pattern. The standard requires some tan, however pale, to be present, as pure black and white is not allowed.

Well-placed white markings dress up the basic coloring. Almost all Pembroke Welsh Corgis have white socks and at least a splash of white on the chest. Some shine with full white collars. On others, a blaze or snippet on the muzzle looks attractive. There is endless variation, and no two Corgis ever seem to be exactly the same. This is much more fun than the solid colors of many other breeds and helps to identify individuals.

Almost all Pembroke Welsh Corgis have white "socks" and at least a little bit of white on the chest.

As with the coat texture, the wrong amount or incorrect placement of the white can be considered a Very Serious Fault by the standard. "Mismarks" are dogs with any white on the back between the withers and tail, on the sides between the elbows and back of the hindquarters or above an imaginary horizontal line drawn from the elbow to the stifle, or on the ears. "Whitelies" have a white body with red or dark markings, sometimes big spots, and are rare.

A final Very Serious Color Fault is Bluie. The colored portions of the coat have a distinct bluish or smoky cast. Tricolored Bluies are steel gray. However, the gene for the Bluie has all but disappeared, and many Corgi fanciers have never seen a Bluie.

GAIT

Free and smooth. Forelegs should reach well forward, without too much lift, in unison with the driving action of the hind legs. The correct shoulder assembly and well-fitted elbows allow the long, free stride in front. Viewed from the front, legs do not move in exact parallel planes, but incline slightly inward to compensate for shortness of leg and width of chest. Hind legs should drive well under the body and move on a line with the forelegs, with hocks turning neither in nor out. Feet must travel parallel to the line of motion with no tendency to swing out, cross over, or interfere with each other. Short, choppy movement, rolling or high-stepping gait, close or overly wide coming or going, are incorrect. This is a herding dog, which must have the agility, freedom of movement, and endurance to do the work for which he was developed.

It is a joy to behold a well-balanced Corgi trotting purposefully along on a loose lead. The ears are laid back, the head is held fairly low, the topline is level and those short legs work with strength and efficiency. Good movement looks effortless. He could go on all day without tiring!

TEMPERAMENT

Although the standard is limited in its description of the desired temperament of the breed, of course emotional stability, self-confidence and enthusiasm for life are of prime importance. Curiosity, intelligence, inventiveness, humor, sensitivity, trainability, loyalty and affection are all typical of a Corgi's wonderful mind. Chapter 3 will expand on the various aspects of the Corgi personality in depth. As with the physical attributes of the dog, the key word is balance. An ideal Pembroke Welsh Corgi has an all-encompassing overall balance.

The **Pembroke Welsh Corgi's** Ancestry

The origins of the Welsh Corgi from Pembrokeshire in southern Wales and that of her counterpart, the Welsh Corgi from more northerly Cardiganshire, are intertwined and anything but clear. What is certain is that they have been flourishing on the homesteads in the Welsh hills for many centuries. As for when and how they got there in the first place, several theories have been put forth.

The History of the Pembroke Welsh Corgi

IN MYTH AND LEGEND

A charming legend has been passed down through the generations regarding the Corgi's history. According to the myth, children

18

playing in the woods found two puppies with foxy faces and short legs and brought them home. The grownups said they were gifts from the fairies who used them to draw their carriages or as fairy steeds. When the children's dogs got older, they were helpful with many tasks on the farm and with the livestock, just as Corgis are today. As proof of their connection to the spirit world, Pembroke Corgis still carry the marks of the fairy saddle on their backs.

The "fairy saddle" pattern on the Corgi's back has perpetuated the legend that the breed has a mythical connection to the spirit world.

THE BREED'S HISTORICAL CONTEXT

The first historical mention of what may have been a Corgi, however, was in the Laws of Hywel Dda, King of South Wales, codified around A.D. 920. Here, a herdsman's cur (or dog) was differentiated from a house cur and watch cur. As some believe the Corgi was the only type of herding dog established in Wales until the 1800s, the Laws might authenticate the Corgi's existence in the tenth century. However, the reference could have been to any sort of dog the farmer used for herding, as in those days most dogs had to have many talents to earn their keep.

A better developed, if not actually substantiated, theory was outlined by W. Lloyd-Thomas in a series of articles first published in 1935 in *Pure-Bred Dogs—American Kennel Gazette*. It is generally accepted that the Pembroke and the Cardigan Welsh Corgi stem from entirely different stock. Pembrokes descend from the Northern Spitz group (such as the Siberian Husky) with characteristic prick ears, pointed muzzle, thick coat and a tail that curls over the back. Cardigans according to this theory are members of the Tekel group, represented by long, low dogs like the Basset Hound or Dachshund.

Lloyd-Thomas placed Cardigan-like dogs in the Welsh hills as early as 1200 B.C. where they accompanied the migrating Celtic people. The ancestors of the Pembroke were traced to arrive in Wales with the Flemish weavers around A.D. 1107 Eventually, according to Lloyd-Thomas, the drop-eared "original" Corgi in Cardiganshire was refined by interbreeding with other varieties of herding dogs. This took place after 1875, which marks the change from pasturing cattle on common land to the use of property boundaries. The Corgi's skill at chasing neighboring farmers' cows out of a favored grazing area of the common land was to be replaced by herding abilities of other breeds aimed at rounding up

Though significantly smaller in size than the farm animals that she herds, the Pembroke Welsh Corgi possesses the ability to do so with style.

and confining cattle. Many years earlier, the body shape and length of leg of the Pembrokeshire dog was influenced by her northern neighbor thanks to occasional Cardis brought down and sold to the southern farmers. Supposedly, the Pembrokes never were taken up to Cardiganshire. In any case, it is true that the two breeds began to look more and more alike.

A second theory was offered by another student of both breeds, Clifford Hubbard. He suggested that the Vikings from Norway brought Spitz-like dogs with them on their forays to Wales in the ninth and tenth centuries. It is true that a Nordic breed, the Vallhund, looks very much like a grayish, long-legged Corgi. If the Vallhund was crossed with native dogs in south

Wales, the result might have been similar to the Pembroke, especially if there was added influence from the Flemish dogs—possibly early Schipperkes or Pomeranians. The flaw with this theory is that modern Vallhunds come from Sweden, not Norway (home of the Vikings), and they are the wrong color. But they can have natural bobtails, which seems to be evidence of a connection between them and the Pembroke.

The most recent theory is postulated by Iris Coombe, a researcher on the pastoral breeds. In a book published in 1987, *Herding Dogs, Their Origins and Development in Britain,* she discusses the eighth century Scandinavian people who regularly visited the seacoast of western Britain to procure birds, eggs and feathers from the heavily populated rookeries. They probably brought with them dogs similar to Lundehunds, another Spitz-like breed that was particularly adept at working through the rocky terrain in quest of birds. Lundehunds, or Puffin Dogs, are an ancient and pure Celtic breed that resemble Pembroke Corgis, except for their long legs. What is more, they are the same color. If the Vikings who settled Wales had Lundehunds instead of Vallhunds, and proceeded as Hubbard suggests, the problem of the gray color and point of origin in Hubbard's theory might be resolved.

Mrs. Coombe has learned of a further legacy—as the feather and fowl trade persisted in later centuries, Pembroke Corgis were used to round up and pen poultry and even to drive flocks of large birds to market.

What's in a Name?

The origins of the name *Corgi* are even less clear than the breed's provenance. Again, breed historians have various explanations. Some think that it is derived from the word *cur,* meaning "to watch over" in Welsh. Others credit the Celts for whom *corgi* was their word for "dog." At the time of the Norman Conquest this was corrupted to *curgi* or "cur," meaning any small mongrel. In Wales, the name evolved to include any small cattle dog.

Other scholars hunted through ancient Welsh writings to find *corgi* or *korgi* equivalent to "cur" or "cur dog." Thus, the herdsman's cur would be the Welsh Corgi. Another possibility is that *cor* is Welsh for "dwarf" and *gi* is a word for "dog." In any case, the breed was known mostly as Welsh Curs well into the nineteenth century. Although *corgwyn* is the Welsh plural of "Corgi," the correct spelling for more than one is "Corgis," (no "e").

Coming off the Farm

During the latter part of the 1800s, Corgis were very popular on the Pembrokeshire farms. They began to be exhibited at local agricultural shows under the classification of Cwn Sodli ("heeling dogs"), Heelers and Curs. In 1925, Corgis first appeared at a show under the rules of the English Kennel Club, and some dogs prominent in early pedigrees are recorded as having been present. Pembrokes and Cardigans were shown together. "Rose," the first Pembroke to be registered with the Kennel Club, placed third.

Though these Cardigan Corgis look like their Pembroke cousins, they are, in fact, members of an entirely different breed.

The next twenty years were extremely important in the history of the breed. Knowledgeable breeders of purebred dogs "discovered" and fell under the charms of these small farm dogs. In December of 1925, the Corgi Club was founded in Carmarthen, Pembrokeshire. Naturally, the local members favored the Pembroke breed, so a year later a club for Cardigan enthusiasts was created. Both are still in existence. Each group worked hard to standardize the appearance and type of its breed through careful selective breeding. The first standard for the breed was drawn up in 1925. It was not long before these stylish little dogs began to attract attention. They were officially recognized and given championship status by the Kennel Club in 1928, but lumped together under the heading Welsh Corgis.

PEMBROKES AND CARDIGANS

At one point, there were some hard feelings between the supporters of each breed and gray areas as to which was which. One notable litter produced both a Pembroke and a Cardigan champion. Finally, in 1934, the Kennel Club granted the much desired separate status to each breed. It was obvious that the marked differences between the breeds could not and should not be reconciled. A Cardigan is not a long-tailed Pembroke. During the same year, a three-year-old docking ban that attempted to unify the two breeds was lifted, and Pembrokes became even more uniform in appearance.

Ch. Rozavel Red Dragon was an exemplar of the breed.

A ROYAL BREED

The Pembroke Welsh Corgi was extremely fortunate to come to the attention of Mrs. Thelma Gray (nee Evans), an Englishwoman and owner of Rozavel Kennels. She applied her considerable talent and amazing energy to the development and promotion of the breed both in Britain and overseas. Her Ch. (the abbreviation for champion) Rozavel Red Dragon, born in 1932, is a pillar of the breed, and until just recently was the top producing English sire of all time with thirteen champions to his credit.

*This photo of
Queen Elizabeth
as a young girl
demonstrates
British royalty's
admiration for
the breed.*

Another milestone was the founding of The Welsh Corgi League in England in 1938. Again, Mrs. Gray and her colleagues spearheaded the organization, which remains a dominant force in the Corgi world and which celebrated its Diamond Jubilee in 1998 with international attendance.

It was from Mrs. Gray that the Duke of York, later King George VI, bought a Corgi puppy in 1933 for his two daughters, Elizabeth and Margaret Rose. Since that time, the present Queen Elizabeth II has enjoyed a steady line of Corgis that have given her companionship and support through the rigors of royal life. She tends to them herself and even personally selects the sires of litters that she has bred. After sixty-five years, she certainly is the epitome of breed loyalty!

Needless to say, royal interest in the Pembroke Welsh Corgi had quite an effect on the breed's popularity. Long gone are the days of the Corgi's obscurity on the farms of southern Wales. Members of the breed span the globe and are particularly numerous in several former British territories, most notably Australia and New Zealand.

Traveling to America

While on a trip to London during 1933, Mrs. Lewis Roesler (later Mrs. Edward Renner) chanced upon a show-bound red and white Corgi named Little Madam in Paddington Station. It was love at first sight and the bitch was purchased on the spot. In the spring of 1934, Little Madam and a young dog from a Corgi kennel in Wales returned to Mrs. Roesler's famous Merriedip Old English Sheepdog Kennels in Massachusetts and became the first Pembroke Welsh Corgis to step on American shores. As such, Little Madam and her companion became the first of the breed to be registered with the American Kennel Club. Little Madam later earned her championship.

Other Corgis were soon to take the long ocean voyage, and they found themselves on both coasts. The first American registered Pembroke Welsh Corgi litter was born in 1934. The dam was purchased in Canada and was of Rozavel breeding. Eng. Am. Ch. Sierra Bowhit Pivot won the breed's first all-breed Best in Show in England before he was exported and earned the first American championship. Eventually he settled in California with the well-known American judge Derek Rayne and went on to sire five champions.

In the States, the breed caught on quickly. In February of 1936, at the time of the Westminster Kennel Club show in New York City, the Pembroke Welsh Corgi Club of America (PWCCA) held its first meeting. The PWCCA is the parent club of the breed, and is in charge of developing and maintaining the breed standard. The PWCCA has affiliated member clubs throughout the country, and its annual National Specialty show attracts hundreds of the nation's top Corgis for keen competition. This eminent and active organization is the prime force in the American Corgi world.

Ch. Little Madam of Merriedip, a Bowhit Pepper daughter, one of the first Pembroke Welsh Corgis to be registered with the American Kennel Club, in 1934.

The Breed Today

It is only natural that a tide of British Corgis flowed into America and the other countries while the breed was being established away from the homeland. During the years prior to World War II many excellent kennels came into being on both sides of the Atlantic, and significant bloodlines emerged. Fame within the dog world came to many specimens of excellent quality. Fortunately, the English hiatus during the war did not seriously affect the progress of the breed. English Corgis will always be admired and exported to those seeking their special beauty and heritage.

The American Pembroke Welsh Corgi has flourished as well over the past seven decades. Kennels in all parts of the United States are breeding dogs of lovely quality. Some still infuse their bloodlines from time to time with English imports, but others have been extremely successful working with "all-American" stock. The American Corgi today can figure in with the best that the world has to offer.

The popularity of purebred dogs in general has burgeoned in recent years. The American Kennel Club keeps record of these trends. The Pembroke Welsh Corgi has always ranked between thirty-fourth and thirty-eighth in breed popularity, but the numbers of individual and litter registrations have increased dramatically. The Pembroke is certainly not a rare breed, but is fortunately not a "trendy" breed either. Concerned and conscientious breeders want to keep it that way.

Claims to Fame

In addition to the most famous Corgi owner of them all, Queen Elizabeth, other noteworthy individuals have surrounded themselves with these special little dogs.

WHERE DID DOGS COME FROM?

It can be argued that dogs were right there at man's side from the beginning of time. As soon as human beings began to document their existence, the dog was among their drawings and inscriptions. Dogs were not just friends, they served a purpose: There were dogs to hunt birds, pull sleds, herd sheep, burrow after rats—even sit in laps! What your dog was originally bred to do influences the way it behaves. The American Kennel Club recognizes over 140 breeds, and there are hundreds more distinct breeds around the world. To make sense of the breeds, they are grouped according to their size or function. The AKC has seven groups:

1) Sporting, 2) Working, 3) Herding, 4) Hounds, 5) Terriers, 6) Toys, 7) Nonsporting

Can you name a breed from each group? Here's some help: (1) Golden Retriever; (2) Doberman Pinscher; (3) Collie; (4) Beagle; (5) Scottish Terrier; (6) Maltese; (7) Dalmation. All modern domestic dogs (*Canis familiaris*) are related, however different they look, and are all descended from *Canis lupus*, the gray wolf.

The well-known artist and illustrator, Tasha Tudor, invariably includes sketches of her beloved family of Corgis in her exquisite drawings. Tasha lives in a quaint New England farmhouse surrounded by bountiful gardens, assorted ducks, geese, goats and cats, all of which are depicted in charming detail in her numerous books and greeting cards. "Caleb," a handsome red and white Corgi, is the hero of two fanciful books, *Corgiville Fair* and *The Great Corgiville Kidnapping.* These books are a treat for Corgi fanciers young and old. Several books have been written about Tasha Tudor herself, and all depict her Corgis.

A few of the luminaries said to have owned Pembrokes are the opera singer Beverly Sills, the late Ava Gardner (who was given her last Corgi by Frank Sinatra, her husband at the time), Gregory Peck, French Stewart (an actor on the TV show *Third Rock from the Sun*), Greg Louganis, novelist Stephen King and even France's General Charles de Gaulle. A dog that has done some nice winning recently, Ch. Just Enuff of The Real Thing (call name "Fizz"), was co-owned by Coca-Cola's magnate, Roberto C. Goizueta.

In 1963, the Corgi hit the silver screen with Walt Disney's full-length color adventure film, *Little Dog Lost.* People across the country related to the perils of a Corgi puppy separated from its family. In the end, of course, they were reunited. The "actors" in this drama were clever obedience-trained Corgi ladies owned and handled by Douglas Bundock from California. The Corgi in a more recent film, *The Accidental Tourist,* is a Cardigan. The author of the book from which the film was made, novelist Anne Tyler, owned a Pembroke appropriately named Ernest.

**FAMOUS
OWNERS
OF THE
PEMBROKE
WELSH CORGI**

Queen
Elizabeth II

Tasha Tudor,
Artist/Illustrator

General
Charles de
Gaulle

Ava Gardner
and
Gregory Peck,
Film Stars

French
Stewart,
TV Actor

Beverly Sills,
Opera Singer

Greg
Louganis,
Olympic Diver

Roberto
Goizueta,
Coca-Cola
Executive

Anne Tyler
and Stephen
King, Novelists

chapter 3

The **World** According to the **Pembroke Welsh Corgi**

The mind of the Pembroke Welsh Corgi is special—to know it is to love the breed. To ignore it is a great pity, as it precludes the opportunity to experience a truly wonderful relationship with your dog.

Character Traits

It does not take more than a moment to realize that your Corgi is one smart little fellow. Regardless of age, the alert expression and awareness of his surroundings are immediately obvious. The position of his ears can be subtly changed to register an opinion on just about any subject. Obviously, a Corgi cannot speak to a human, but at the same time, he does not need to. He easily gets his point across with a meaningful glance and body or ear language.

His eyes speak volumes. And do not underestimate his ability to understand almost every word you say or even think. It is not hard to learn how to "read" members of the breed, and to "think dog" is essential to enjoying a Corgi's world.

Energy and Activity

As there aren't any cattle to chase in the average suburban backyard, the Corgi must now devote his ample energies to other activities. And a Corgi loves to be busy exercising or playing. He is always ready for a game of fetch, dashing out and returning to your feet with the prize stuffed in his mouth. Anything will do. A stick from outside, a fuzzy toy, a tennis ball . . . the list of safe toys is endless!

Corgis, having been bred to chase cattle, are full of energy!

Fun, Games and, of Course, Rest

It's great fun to play "rake-it-ball" with the fall leaves or "where-did-that-yellow-thing-go-in-all-this-cold-white-stuff?" in the winter. Most every Corgi can be an avid ballplayer when given the chance. It is a super way to give him the daily exercise he needs when the schedule does not allow time for a long walk. Corgis need to expend energy and thrive in a household with an active lifestyle.

Although he loves to play, the Corgi is not a hyperactive dog constantly demanding more and more action. When it is reading time he will settle down quietly for a short snooze or peacefully pursue the merits of a chew toy or bone. He is a sensible, comfortable companion. (Chapter 4 addresses appropriate items for chewing.)

*Although Corgis
like action, they
also know how to
take five.*

Although they would prefer a yard to run in, many Corgis adjust happily to apartments and life on a leash. It is the quality of the time he gets that counts. A compassionate owner, no matter how sedentary, can devise ways to provide activity and the all-important individual attention a Corgi craves.

WATER BABIES

Although their job description does not call for "aquabatics," most Corgis love to swim. The fascination with water begins at an early age. Some puppies just cannot resist pawing in the water bowl. Next they will be found jumping in every available puddle, which progresses to extended swims in the lake or pond. It is more fun when "frogging" from the shore can be added or someone is kind enough to throw in a retrievable stick or ball. And what dog does not enjoy tearing along the beach barking at the foaming water's edge?

Natural bodies of water are not necessary. The swimming pool will do just fine (although there are fewer frogs). Many a Corgi will jump right in even from a diving board. One notable pool pooch has her own rubber raft for lounging. When she gets too hot, she rolls off for a dip and climbs up the pool's ladder to get out and start all over again. It is crucial, of course, that the dog knows how to get out of the pool and is carefully watched. Pools should be off limits for unsupervised pups.

A Corgi's swimming style determines his stability in the water. Without long legs to lower his center of gravity, he tends to bob about. His chin should rest on the surface, otherwise his rear will sink when he turns. Swimming with people is great sport. It is even worth the effort to herd a sunbather into the water for this joy. Excitement escalates with all the splashing.

More Personality Traits

Corgis are curious. Introduce any new item and he will be on the spot evaluating with sniffing nose, bristling whiskers and probing paw. As soon as he is satisfied as to the meaning of the innovation, he will proceed appropriately. Check out the comfort level and size of the new dog bed. Bark at the box turtle. Avoid the artichoke. He always has to know what is going on. It is hard to sneak anything past a Corgi!

The Corgi is also inventive. To avoid boredom, he will play with his toys in an amusing and creative way. More than one Corgi has figured out that dropping a ball down the stairs is the answer when no one is around to throw it. One little guy perfected his ability to maneuver a soccer ball around the yard for half an hour at a time without ever losing control of it. I know of one Corgi that invented "scooter bone," whereby he stepped on and pushed a bone along with one front paw and barked gleefully at the moving object. The same Corgi used to pounce on the dry dirt with his paws together and squirt up puffs of dust which he practiced biting just for the fun of it!

Corgis are fascinated with water.

Corgis observe their owners closely. If you are about to go out, even without telling him that he is not slated

CHARACTER-
ISTICS OF A
PEMBROKE
WELSH CORGI

Intelligent

Highly
Trainable

Enthusiastic

Companionable

Sensible

Fun-Loving

Affectionate

Alert

to accompany you, he will amble over to his favorite resting spot and flop down in acceptance of his circumstances. He may indeed have read your mind, or perhaps he figured out that you always comb your hair in front of a certain mirror just before you leave on a non-doggy excursion. He knows you very well.

Your Corgi will take his role as a family member very seriously. Some dogs take charge when squabbling siblings need to be separated. They will snuggle up to a teary tot or herd the child away from potential danger. A Corgi will run and bark in a call for help. One Corgi repeatedly pressed himself against his fallen friend, who lives alone, in an effort to boost her to her feet.

Concern extends to other pets as well. A young Corgi alerted his owner that his elderly canine companion had wandered deaf and unseeing out of the safety of the garden. Another dog rushed to protect "his" cat from the over-exuberant advances of a passing puppy. Back on the Welsh farms the Corgi was counted upon to use his brains for the welfare of the other animals.

As is usual with most herding breeds, the Pembroke Welsh Corgi's overall psychological makeup tends toward marked allegiance to one person, the leader of the "pack." A strong bond is formed, and his devotion is shown in many ways. Without being cloying, the Corgi gives honest affection and loves to receive it. He is always right there, happy to be noticed, ready to comfort when spirits are low, in sync with every mood. Rapport between the Corgi and his person is intense, which is why the breed can do exceptionally well in performance events like obedience and agility.

One dog was so in tune with his owner that he gave himself a good shake when he saw the man dripping wet from a trip outside in the rain. The same dog lifted his front leg in the air while he watched his person try to climb over the garden gate. That is Corgi empathy.

A breed that cares this much is also going to be quite sensitive. Hardy as they are, Corgis do not do well with any form of harsh treatment. Should the need arise to reprimand him, a firm "no" and a stern look are usually enough. A Corgi has a tremendous desire to please. With kind treatment and respect, this keenly intelligent dog can be trained to do almost anything. He is quick to learn, so take the opportunity to teach him something positive.

BARKING AND STRANGERS

The Corgi has always been valued as a watchdog. His acute hearing alerts him to unusual sounds, and his big dog bark means business when something is amiss. The Corgi has a variety of barks to suit any occasion, but he does not yap or carry on incessantly. When announcing the arrival of a visitor, he will stop barking as soon as he knows the person is welcome. Some Corgis are reserved with strangers, but once they have been introduced, most happily greet a new friend.

A well-adjusted Corgi makes an ideal house pet. His weatherproof coat needs relatively little grooming to keep it attractive. A quick once-over with a towel is appreciated after a damp walk, and residual dirt will drop out as the coat dries. (The wise owner chooses where this occurs.) Also, the coat does shed, only lightly all the time, but completely some of the time, and so this is not a breed for the fastidious. More about necessary coat care will be covered in Chapter 6, which addresses grooming.

A DOG'S SENSES

Sight: With their eyes located farther apart than ours, dogs can detect movement at a greater distance than we can, but they can't see as well up close. They can also see better in less light, but they can't distinguish many colors.

Sound: Dogs can hear about four times better than we can, and they can hear high-pitched sounds especially well. Their ancestors, the wolves, howled to let other wolves know where they were; our dogs do the same, but they have a wider range of vocalizations, including barks, whimpers, moans and whines.

Smell: A dog's nose is his greatest sensory organ. His sense of smell is so great he can follow a trail that's weeks old, detect odors diluted to one-millionth the concentration we'd need to notice them, even sniff out a person underwater!

Taste: Dogs have fewer taste buds than we do, so they're likelier to try anything—and usually do, which is why it's especially important for their owners to monitor their food intake. Dogs are omnivores, which means they eat meat as well as vegetable matter like grasses and weeds.

Touch: Dogs are social animals and love to be petted, groomed and played with.

Interacting with Other Animals and Kids

CORGIS AND OTHER DOMESTIC ANIMALS

On the Welsh farms, the Pembroke Corgi naturally involved himself with all kinds of domestic animals. Today, the breed is a favorite of equestrians across the country. Corgis seem to have a special, calming way around the horses, neither fearing nor annoying them. Cats and Corgis can be a good combination, too, with the formation of true friendships between the animals. Although generalizations can be made, ultimately it depends on the individual Corgi.

Corgis and kitties will not fight like cats and dogs.

Corgis are fun when there's more than one!

CORGIS AND OTHER CORGIS

Corgis are such charming dogs that owning one often leads to acquiring another. This is fine. In fact, two Corgis are much more than the sum of one and one—to watch their dog-to-dog antics will bring a smile to any face. In addition, two are seldom more trouble to care for than one. However, one Corgi of each sex is by far the best combination. While many well-organized multi-Corgi households do exist harmoniously, these dogs frequently do not get along as well with others of the same sex. Proper socialization from puppyhood teaches them good behavior in a crowd of other dogs and is a must. Undisciplined dogs can be aggressive to other canines, especially toward other males.

*Kids and Corgis
love each other!*

CORGIS AND KIDS

And how will your dog get along with children? A Corgi that has been treated with kindness and respect by the young of our own species will respond with obvious enjoyment, loyalty and tolerance. He will love kids. However, he will not tolerate mean or hurtful behavior and will leave the scene or even make his point clear in a less gracious manner. It is essential that an adult insist on gentleness toward the dog from both their own children and other young folks.

It should be noted that the Corgi's innate herding instinct is often expressed by nipping at flying heels. This is not acceptable, especially if the heels wear size 5 Keds! It is not difficult to train the dog out of this behavior, but definitely necessary. Training the children not to encourage the dog's inclination is equally important.

Welcome to
the World of
the Pembroke
Welsh Corgi

*Never underesti-
mate the mind of
a Corgi.*

Act as a Leader, Your Corgi Will Follow

If the Corgi has a downside, it stems from the fact that he is super-smart and has a strong sense of his own being. A willful chap can and sometimes does get the "upper paw" on an owner who cannot stay one pace ahead of him. A Corgi needs a leader he respects, or he

might assume the position himself. As cute as his antics may be, he must learn at once *what* is appropriate and *who* is boss. A Corgi is not for someone who is unwilling to accept this challenge.

More Information on Pembroke Welsh Corgis

NATIONAL BREED CLUB

The Pembroke Welsh Corgi Club of America, Inc.
Joan Gibson Reid,
Corresponding Secretary
9589 Sheldon Road
Elk Grove, CA 95624

The PWCCA has an informative Web page on the Internet. The address is http://www.pembrokecorgi.org

The Corresponding Secretary of the PWCCA will send an illustrated and informative brochure on the breed with a list of publications plus the names and addresses of members/ breeders in your geographical area. She can also direct you to the regional Corgi club nearest you.

BOOKS

Cole, Margaret A. *The Welsh Corgi.* Edinburgh: John Bartholomew & Son Ltd., 1981.

Gray, Thelma. *The Welsh Corgi.* London: Watmoughs, Ltd., 1936 and 1946.

Harper, Deborah S. *The New Complete Pembroke Welsh Corgi.* New York: Howell Book House, 1994.

Hubbard, Clifford L.B. *The Pembrokeshire Corgi.* The Dog Lover's Library. London: Nicholson & Watson, 1952.

Lister-Kaye, Charles. *The Popular Welsh Corgi.* London: Popular Dogs Publishing Co., Ltd., 1954, 1956, 1959, 1961, 1965. In 1968 this book was revised and enlarged by Dickie Albin, with a seventh edition in 1970, and the volume was retitled *The Welsh Corgi.* An eighth edition was printed in 1974.

Sargent, Mary Gay and Deborah S. Harper. *The Complete Pembroke Welsh Corgi.* New York: Howell Book House, 1979.

Tudor, Tasha. *Corgiville Fair.* New York: Thomas Y. Crowell Co., 1971.

MAGAZINES

Pembroke Welsh Corgi Newsletter

The official magazine of the Pembroke Welsh Corgi Club of America, Inc. As editors frequently change, contact the club's Corresponding Secretary for the current address of this publication.

Each of the regional Affiliate Clubs publishes its own newsletter. Some of these are outstanding and offer commentary on a wide range of current Corgi activities.

VIDEOS

The Pembroke Welsh Corgi. New York: The American Kennel Club, 1994.

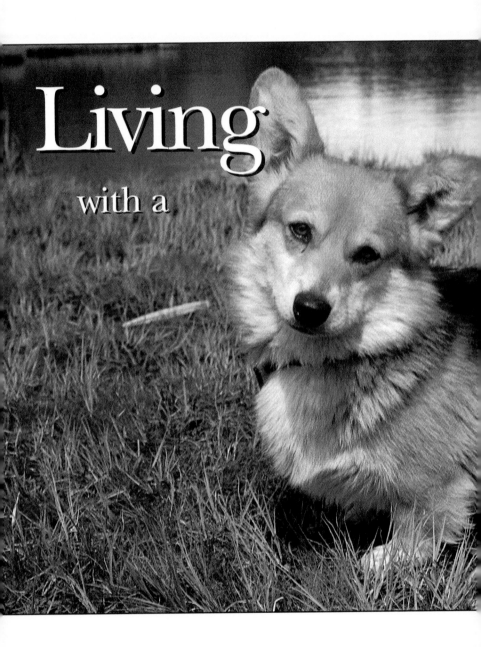

Living

with a

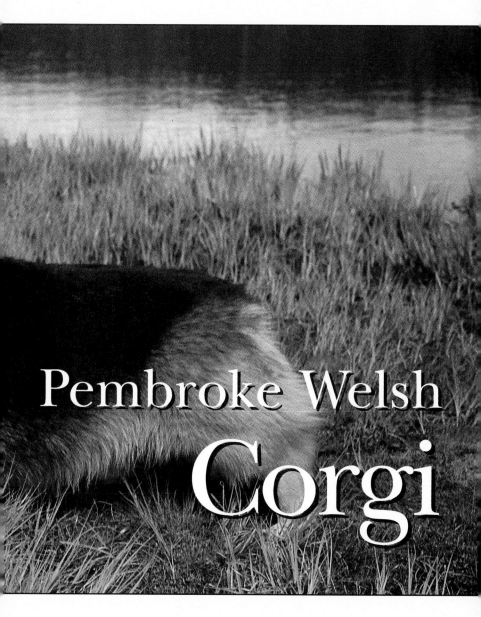

part two

Pembroke Welsh Corgi

chapter 4

Bringing Your

Pembroke Welsh
Corgi Home

It usually works out for the best if you can purchase your Corgi puppy from a reputable private breeder who has spent a lot of time and effort to produce well-socialized, healthy puppies of good quality. This person can help you select the perfect puppy in the litter to suit your particular lifestyle, and will be an ongoing source of assistance and information whenever you need it.

Getting Acquainted

The first few weeks in her new home are a most critical period in your Corgi's life. There is much to learn and many changes from the early days with her littermates. To ensure that the transition goes smoothly and that both puppy and new owner start off on the right foot, a little preplanning is advisable.

40

Most puppies are between 8 and 12 weeks old when they leave home. By this age they have had enough time to learn the basics of acceptable doggy behavior from their dam and siblings. Now they must cope with human expectations. Little puppies are still babies and need clear and consistent guidelines to help them adjust to the life of their new family.

Pembroke puppies can win your heart instantaneously, but choose carefully! Make sure you pick the right dog for you.

Preparing for Your Pup

Before you bring your Corgi home, a few decisions need to be made. Where are you going to keep this adorable and rambunctious ball of fur until she can be trained to be the dog of your dreams?

Where is she going to sleep? Where will you keep her when you go out and have to leave her behind? Where is she supposed to relieve herself? Will she have free access to the sofa? Who is going to feed her and where? And most important, is she coming into your life when you can spare the extra time to enjoy her puppyhood and teach her the ways of your world? Plan in advance, not on the spur of the moment.

ACCOMMODATIONS FOR A PUPPY

Your dog needs to start out in a restricted area of your home that is easy to keep clean and safe for an inquisitive Corgi puppy. A portable wire pen is ideal, especially if it is set up in the kitchen or family room where the action is. Corgis are not happy when relegated to a

Living with a
Pembroke
Welsh Corgi

cold garage or lonely basement. A 2-foot-high wire mesh baby gate across a doorway also works well to keep her confined to the kitchen or a mudroom. These gates are convenient, easy to step over and do not cause the puppy to feel isolated the way a solid door does. Wire can't be chewed to bits and so it is better than plastic, wood or string, which can all can be destroyed.

PUPPY-PROOF YOUR HOME!

Your dog's surroundings must be "puppy-proofed." Valuable table legs and fluffy pillows should not become irresistible temptations. Many houseplants are harmful if ingested, and Corgi-gardeners are not to be encouraged. Electrical cords should be arranged so that they are out of reach, and your Corgi must not be left unattended where plug-in items are necessary. Household chemicals belong behind secure cupboard doors. Common sense applied goes a long way to safeguard Miss Puppy.

Puppies are curious, and it is in their nature to bite and tear at anything. Be sure not only to protect your furniture and other possessions from them, but to protect them from hazards in and around the house as well.

Basically, the object is to control your dog's environment until she can distinguish between right and wrong activities. It is decidedly unwise to let a new puppy "have the run of the house" upon first arrival. Bad habits are quickly acquired and hard to break. It is best to start small and then gradually expand the horizons as training and bladder control progress. In the early stages, she should be brought into the living room only for brief periods under the watchful eye of an adult. Chapter 8 outlines a plan of action for housebreaking and other desirable accomplishments.

Crates and Bedding

There are many comfy dog beds on the market. Even a cardboard box will suffice. But as all puppies chew, be prepared to find any pillows shredded. Imitation sheepskin as bedding is fairly sturdy, washable and has dog appeal. Whatever the choice, your dog should have a soft spot of her own where she can sleep in peace.

CRATES

Wild canines, especially puppies, spend a great deal of time in a cozy, secure den. You can provide a "civilized" version of this haven by offering your dog a crate to sleep in. Simultaneously, a crate can help exercise some control over your dog's whereabouts when necessary. If you never have used a dog crate before, it helps to apply the proper word "crate" as opposed to "cage," which can summon negative overtones. Corgis love crates. If your dog is introduced to her crate in a positive way, she will invariably use it as her own room, with a treasured toy or for a short snooze. Just supply a soft, washable blanket or towel, leave the door open and watch. The crate can be placed in your dog's corner of the kitchen or wherever you have set up a spot for her. And of course, the closed crate is perfect for housebreaking, sleeping and travel.

Your dog may fuss a bit at first when the crate door is shut. Each time you put her in, supply a treat and a favorite toy. Tell her she is a good girl, and disregard her clamor to escape. She will soon settle down. If you let her out when she cries, she will have "one up" on you . . . not a good position with a Corgi. You make all the decisions, not her. Let her know this and she will respect you for it.

HOUSEHOLD DANGERS

Curious puppies and inquisitive dogs get into trouble not because they are bad, but simply because they want to investigate the world around them. It's our job to protect our dogs from harmful substances, like the following:

IN THE HOUSE

cleaners, especially pine oil

perfumes, colognes, aftershaves

medications, vitamins

office and craft supplies

electric cords

chicken or turkey bones

chocolate

some house and garden plants, like ivy, oleander and poinsettia

IN THE GARAGE

antifreeze

garden supplies, such as snail and slug bait, pesticides, fertilizers, mouse and rat poisons

---

CRATE TYPES

Crates can be made of heavy wire, plastic/fiberglass or wood. Wire is cooler in warm weather. Fiberglass is required by airlines and is snug and lighter than wood. A variety of models may be found in pet shops or wholesale animal supply catalogs. It is important to get the right size for an adult Corgi. A crate that is too big is no better than one that is too small. The dimensions should be approximately 27 inches long by 22 inches high by 17 inches wide. A big male might appreciate a little more room, but the crate loses its appeal as a den if it is too spacious.

RESPONSIBLE USE OF THE CRATE

Crates are wonderful for all involved, but their use must not be abused. Be sure the dog gets a chance to exercise and/or eliminate before confinement. No dog, a puppy in particular, should be locked in a crate for extensive periods of time during the day. Forced confinement is destructive to the dog's mind.

A fenced yard is the best way to contain your dog.

Outdoor Safety

With the advent of leash laws and high-speed motor vehicles, the general public has, fortunately, an increased awareness of the folly of letting a dog "run loose." It is irresponsible to usher a dog out the front door after breakfast to fend for herself. Perhaps on large properties and under reliable voice control a dog can frolic or work unfettered in safety, but for peace of mind, a fenced yard is best.

BAD IDEAS . . .

A freestanding chain-link kennel run behind a detached garage is out of sight but out of mind and heart as well, and is not a happy place for a Corgi. And being tied up is miserable for any dog.

. . . And Good Ones

There are, however, humane and painless ways to keep your dog in one place. Fortunately, Corgis have short legs. Wire fencing that is only 3 feet high is enough to contain them. With a little ingenuity, and at minor expense, an adequate pen can be arranged in just about any yard. The perfect setup is a fenced area large enough for the Corgi to be able to get up to running speed. Access should be via a convenient door, so the dog can remain close to the house while resting outdoors.

A leash is an absolute necessity when walking your dog.

Walking the Dog

Not everyone has a backyard or is able to provide the security of fencing. For these owners, walking the dog is a way of life. Corgis can thrive with the guaranteed bonding time that leash walking brings. If you use a retractable leash, your dog's walk will be a little more adventurous for her. Nonetheless, a good run in a safe place is always appreciated.

Equipment

Additional precautions must be provided for your little Corgi until she learns the routine. Someone needs to keep an eye on her activities outside as well as inside. There are many dangerous temptations just outside your front door.

Puppy's First Collar

The best type of first collar for a Corgi puppy is made of soft, flat nylon webbing and is fastened with a buckle. A cat collar is fine for a tiny puppy. As your dog grows, she will graduate to a flat nylon web or leather collar, not more than ¾-inch wide. The metal loop will hold her veterinary tags and most importantly,

45

identification. Be sure that the collar is just tight enough so that it does not pull over the ears, but remains loose around the neck. Check the collar's fit as your dog grows to be sure that it doesn't get too tight. Also, keep in mind that many people do not leave a collar on their Corgi, as it eventually makes an unattractive indentation in the ruff. Instead, the collar goes on only during a walk.

PUPPY ESSENTIALS

Your new puppy will need:

food bowl

water bowl

collar

leash

ID tag

bed

crate

toys

grooming supplies

GEAR FOR WALKING

For walks, your Corgi needs to accept a leash and collar. Leashes for Corgis are sized appropriately. Often, nylon web collars come with matching 5- to 6-foot leashes. A lead favored by many Corgi owners is $\frac{1}{4}$-inch latigo leather, 6 feet in length. A very light snap on the end will be sufficient. For a retractable lead, select one that is 26 feet in length for a dog under 30 pounds. Although Corgis are strong dogs, they do not need heavy-duty collars and leads (and puppies look pitiful with equipment fit for a Boxer!). Another choice is a nylon braid with rings on each end. This type of collar is excellent as it does not tangle in the neck hair. For an adult, the length to select is 16 inches. The sensitive Corgi can easily be trained not to pull with just a light touch on the lead. A word of warning: Choke collars should never be left on after the walk. Accidents can occur.

Other Supplies

In addition to a leash, your dog will need many other supplies in order to ensure that she remains happy and healthy. The following are necessary items that your dog can't do without.

FOR FEEDING

Your dog is going to need her own bowls for food and water. Bowls made of stainless steel or heavy crockery are better than plastic (which can be chewed or some-times may even bleach the nose). A 1-quart size is big enough for even the largest adult Corgi.

FOR GROOMING

For keeping your dog's coat neat and clean, a good quality steel comb with thick and thin spacing of the teeth is essential. A very fine-toothed flea comb will often come in handy as well. A natural bristle brush and guillotine-style nail clippers round out all that is actually necessary to keep the Corgi looking her best. In Chapter 6, grooming will be discussed in full detail.

FOR CURBING YOUR DOG

Another useful item for any doggy household to have is a pooper-scooper. An old-fashioned coal scoop (which can be purchased at a hardware store) and a paint stick certainly does the trick, but mini-shovels and rakes with long handles make this necessary daily chore easier.

Selecting Toys and Chewies

All puppies go through a "bitey" stage in which they appear to be little more than fur-trimmed mouths. An ample supply of chew toys should be on hand to satiate the puppy's natural urge to exercise her erupting adult teeth.

CHEW TOYS

Homemade playthings are free. An old root or knotted rope, an empty paper towel roll or egg carton, or a knotted sock will fascinate a puppy. Rawhide items are popular, but be careful that the softened, slimy pieces are not swallowed whole—they can choke a puppy. Other parts of animals are sold for dogs to chew. Cow hooves, pig ears, pork snouts . . . the dogs love them (even if the owners are revolted). (Although one has to wonder about the safety of the chemicals used to preserve these items.) Still another option is hard nylon toys, which come in a variety of shapes and flavors. Lengths of knotted rope are amusing and washable.

Corgis enjoy gnawing on a bone, but the wrong kind can splinter and injure the dog's mouth or digestive tract. (Bones should never be given as food.) Hard, natural marrow bones are the only ones that are safe and long lasting. These can be purchased from a pet supply source or from the butcher. The only acceptable fresh bone is cut from the shank of a beef leg bone, does not have any portion of the knuckle attached, is at least 1½ inches long and the bone itself is about ¼ inch thick. There are good reasons for these specifications. Give no other type of bone. Ever!

When your dog starts teething, she'll want to chew everything in sight. To prevent her from doing so, supply her with a good number of chew toys.

OTHER TOYS

The array of available fuzzy toys and colorful latex or vinyl squeakies is mind boggling. Mooing cows, soft sculpture hamburgers, prickly hedgehogs, you name it. These delights are just as much for the amusement of the owner as for the canine recipient. Avoid toys with small items (such as embedded eyes) that can be plucked out and swallowed. And be extremely careful with the squeakers. Corgis are adept at extracting them in a flash. If a vinyl or latex toy is being demolished, remove it. Indigestible foreign objects in the tummy equal a trip to the vet.

TOYS TO AVOID

In addition to the problem chewies mentioned above, there are other objects and toys that shouldn't be given to your puppy. Some behaviorists believe that tug toys promote aggression and possessiveness and advise against playing tug-of-war games with a dog. Moreover, your puppy cannot distinguish your valuables from trash. Do not, for example, offer a discarded shoe. Your dog won't know a castoff from your party pumps. Needless to say, anything left lying about on the floor is fair game to the puppy, so it behooves you to be tidy.

Create a Routine

Every dog thrives on routine: when to get up, when to go out, when to eat and where, when it's bedtime. Doing the same thing at approximately the same time every day provides a comfortable continuity and reduces stress. Your Corgi will benefit from a structured day. Her schedule might include trips outside first thing in the morning, last thing at night, after each meal, after each nap during the day and whatever time in between that she looks as if she needs to relieve herself. Puppies between 3 and 6 months of age should be fed three times a day, and be given a biscuit at bedtime. If the baby is only 8 weeks old, four meals a day is appropriate. Once she reaches 6 months, twice a day is fine until, at about a year, that can be reduced. Your dog should be fed at regular times each day and in the same place. Food and feeding will be discussed in the next chapter.

When planning a schedule for your Corgi, be sure to allow plenty of time for her to sleep. Puppies play hard and then drop. This downtime is when most of the growing takes place. Do not disturb! A puppy that is constantly revved up in play and never allowed to simmer down and rest becomes a neurotic, hyper adult.

SET THE RULES FROM THE START

Corgis, being the clever little creatures they are, need to learn straight off that no back talk is allowed. A Corgi with the "upper paw" can become a tyrant. Growling is not cute at any age. Do not let the puppy get away with anything that you would not like a grown dog to do. If your Corgi resists being handled or snarls and nips, sternly say "No!" and hold her gently but firmly. Act calmly as she carries on, and put her down only when she has quieted. Never allow your Corgi to get her way through bad behavior. Do this when she is young, and she will be easy to handle under difficult circumstances when she grows up. As always, you make the decisions.

BUILDING A BOND

One hears a lot these days about bonding with pets. During your dog's first weeks, it is essential that she learn to trust you and develop the rapport that is the greatest joy between dog and person. Right away, make time to sit quietly (preferably on the floor) with her. Stroke her softly and speak to her in calm tones, perhaps while combing her gently. Let her drift off, snuggled against your leg. The soothing serenity you create for her abides in her Corgi mind. With you she has no fears, no anxiety. She will want you as her own special friend.

chapter 5

Feeding Your Pembroke Welsh Corgi

The old adage "you are what you eat" doesn't only apply to humans, it applies to Pembroke Welsh Corgis, too. A dog that has enjoyed a diet of nutritious, wholesome food, fresh air and exercise will sport a coat that glistens in

the sun, firm flesh and an enthusiastic outlook on life. So what is on the menu?

Dog Food

All dog foods are not created equal. The primary ingredients of some food is ground corn, wheat or rice, while others use chicken, beef or lamb and animal by-products as the main ingredient. They might also include meat meal and additives, preservatives and vitamin/mineral packets. The ingredients, as well as the percentage of crude protein, crude fat, crude fiber and moisture are on the label. You can learn to decipher this material, but for most people it is hard to know which bag or can to select. The study of canine nutrition is very complex.

WHAT TO LOOK FOR . . .

A good bet is to seek out one of the excellent brands manufactured by a reputable company and usually sold at specialty pet food stores. Look for wording on the label that says this food is formulated to meet nutritional levels established through feeding trials by the AAFCO (Association of American Feed Control Officials). This group has created Dog Food Nutrient Profiles that define the minimum (and sometimes maximum) daily requirement of each essential nutrient in an ideal canine diet. You then can rely on the overall balance of the product even though the quality of the ingredients may be undetermined. In keeping with the current trend toward health food, many new brands have exceptionally pure, wholesome, all natural ingredients.

> **TO SUPPLEMENT OR NOT TO SUPPLEMENT?**
>
> If you're feeding your dog a diet that's correct for her developmental stage and she's alert, healthy looking and neither over- nor underweight, you don't need to add supplements. These include table scraps as well as vitamins and minerals. In fact, a growing puppy is in danger of developing musculoskeletal disorders by oversupplementation. If you have any concerns about the nutritional quality of the food you're feeding, discuss them with your veterinarian.

You may have to pay a bit more, but it is worth it to feed your friend well. A Corgi deserves the best.

. . . AND WHAT TO AVOID

Knowing what should *not* be included in your Corgi's diet is just as important as (if not more important than) knowing what *should* be. Avoid soy meal, which is a cheap source of protein and has been linked to some health troubles. Some dogs do not assimilate ground corn well. Look for natural sources of nutrition such as vitamins A and E and avoid foods that contain BHA, BHT, ethoxyquin or chemicals. Stay away from generic brands. Their only merit is a low price. Studies have shown they actually can lead to serious nutritional deficiencies.

Types of Food

There are three basic categories into which virtually all commercial dog foods fall—dry, semi-moist and canned. Each provides the needed nutrients, just in a different consistency.

Dry Food

Dry food is available in meal form, baked biscuits broken into bits (kibbled) or pressed into a variety of small, shaped morsels. Some brands make gravy when water is added. Others are extruded and sprayed with fat to enhance the flavor and palatability. Dry food is economical, easy to store and a basic feed.

Generally speaking, Corgis can get along eating just dry food, but the addition of a few spoonfuls of a balanced canned food is a popular practice. Pour some hot water on the dry food to soak for a moment before adding the canned. This creates an appetizing aroma, and it is better to have the kibble absorbing water instead of stomach juices.

Semi-Moist Food

Semi-moist food is really designed with the owner in mind rather than the dog. It is colored to resemble raw meat (dogs are color blind) and comes in cellophane wrapped meal-sized patties

---

HOW TO READ THE DOG FOOD LABEL

With so many choices on the market, how can you be sure you're feeding the right food to your dog? The information's all there on the label—if you know what you're looking for.

Look for the nutritional claim right up top. Is the food "100% nutritionally complete?" If so, it's for nearly all life stages; "growth and maintenance," on the other hand, is for early development; puppy foods are marked as such, as are senior foods.

Ingredients are listed in descending order by weight. The first three or four ingredients will tell you the bulk of what the food contains. Look for the highest-quality ingredients, like meats and grains, to be among them.

The Guaranteed Analysis tells you what level of protein, fat, fiber and moisture are in the food, in that order. While these numbers are meaningful, they won't tell you much about the quality of the food. Nutritional value is in the dry matter, not the moisture content. In many ways, seeing is believing.

If your dog has bright eyes, a shiny coat, a good appetite and a good energy level, chances are his diet's fine. Your dog's breeder and your veterinarian are good sources of advice if you're still confused.

or chunks. As a rule, semi-moist food contains high levels of sugar, salt and antidessicants. For proper nutrition, this form of manufactured dog food is not recommended.

Canned Food

Of the three types of commercial fare, canned food is probably the most expensive. Many brands are scientifically developed to provide a well-balanced diet with all the necessary components for adequate nutrition. Others contain only one ingredient, such as meat, and are designed to be fed in conjunction with another sort of balanced food. All have a substantial percentage of moisture (water). Most dogs appear to find canned food quite tasty.

Bowls are usually used for eating.

SPECIAL FORMULAS

Most large dog food companies offer products specifically formulated for dogs of different ages and levels of activity. Puppies have more demanding nutritional requirements than adults. The obese dog needs fewer calories than an active hunting companion. The owner should select from "puppy," "maintenance," "senior" and "lite" foods to suit her dog's particular lifestyle.

SUPPLEMENTS AND ADDITIVES

Dog food companies and a great many veterinarians insist that there is no need to add vitamin and mineral supplements to commercially prepared dog food. Their concern is that the nutritional balance of the product will be disturbed. It takes considerable knowledge to properly supplement your dog's diet with vitamins and minerals. When not administered in precise ratios and amounts, they can be detrimental instead of helpful. However, the effectiveness of these nutrients included in the manufacture of commercial dog rations may be compromised during processing, and Corgis may profit from the addition of a balanced vitamin/mineral complex to their diet. The key word is "balanced." Pet food stores or your veterinarian can suggest specific brands that will be best for your Corgi.

Sometimes a dog's coat appears dry and lackluster—insufficient fatty acids in his diet may be the problem. There are several good products that address the dog's inability to synthesize the linoleic acid needed for healthy skin and coats. A few drops of these each day will work wonders.

Fresh Foods

Fresh food can be added to the basic diet in small amounts. They supply the beneficial enzymes found in raw, natural foods that are destroyed by cooking. Corgis enjoy small pieces of raw vegetables, apples, bananas, and other noncitrus fruits. You can also add cooked chicken or fish or raw hamburger. Table scraps are okay in moderation. Egg yolks are easily digestible and a super source of protein—but note that whole eggs must be cooked before serving. Cottage cheese is also a good nutritional source. Growing puppies, pregnant and nursing bitches, convalescent dogs and those stressed with a heavy show schedule all need these extra additives for optimum condition. Once again, to maintain the desired proper balanced diet, no more than 25 percent of any meal should be one of these "special items."

Water

Although it's not a food, the most important nutritional item to offer to your dog is an adequate supply of water, which must be made available at all times. Animals can survive for a long time in adverse conditions without food, but they will perish without fresh water. It may be necessary to provide several water bowls, outside and inside, and do not forget to wash them often.

Feeding During Different Stages

A dog requires different nutrients, different amounts of fat and different rations of food during the various stages of his life. The following are some tips on how to feed your growing dog appropriately.

FEEDING A PUPPY

When you picked up your pup from the breeder's, you probably were given an information sheet telling what, how much and when he was used to eating. Ideally, you were sent home with a few day's supply of your puppy's food. Follow the breeder's instructions closely to minimize the jolt to your dog's tender life. If you feel you would like to change the menu (perhaps to upgrade it), do so very gradually over several days' time so that his tummy will not be upset. Mix the two foods over time, gradually decreasing the old and increasing the new.

The average 2- to 3-month old Corgi puppy will eat about ⅓ to ½ of a cup (dry measure) of dry kibble per meal. Warm water and about 1 tablespoon of ground meat, cottage cheese or yogurt should be added in order to moisten it. A vitamin/mineral supplement, if you are providing one, should be added once a day. While he is still little, he needs this amount

---

HOW MANY MEALS A DAY?

Individual dogs vary in how much they should eat to maintain a desired body weight—not too fat, but not too thin. Puppies need several meals a day, while older dogs may only need one. Determine how much food keeps your adult dog looking and feeling his best. Then decide how many meals you want to feed with that amount. Like us, most dogs love to eat, and offering two meals a day is more enjoyable for them. If you're worried about overfeeding, make sure you measure correctly and abstain from adding tidbits to the meals.

Whether you feed one or two meals, only leave your dog's food out for the amount of time it takes him to eat it—10 minutes, for example. Freefeeding (when food's available any time) and leisurely meals encourage picky eating. Don't worry if your dog doesn't finish all his dinner in the allotted time. He'll learn he should.

---

three times daily—morning, noon and night. When he and his tummy begin to grow, increase the daily amount. At about 5 or 6 months of age, the noon meal can be discontinued. Continue feeding two equal meals until he is a year old and out of puppyhood. After his first birthday, switch from the "puppy" formula to adult "maintenance" food.

FEEDING AN ADULT

Once your dog has reached the 1-year mark, he can thrive on one meal a day but, with Corgis, it works well to continue feeding twice a day. Select a time in either the morning or evening when you can consistently provide his main meal. (Morning is really best so that he has a full tummy during the daylight hours.) Then, give a small meal in the evening. This arrangement is particularly good if you have more than one dog, as it prevents periods of hunger that could, in turn, lead to unpleasant interaction.

The proper amount to offer an average adult Corgi is between ⅔ of a cup and 1 cup of dry dog chow (dry measure) in the morning and only ¼ cup in the evening. As always, in the morning, moisten dry food with water before you add a few tablespoons of canned or fresh additions. The small evening portion can be fed dry. Stick to your schedule and do not fall victim to those pleading eyes. Snacks between meals have the same effect on Corgis as they do on people.

Water is the most important element in your dog's diet.

DIETING DOGGIES AND PICKY PUPPIES

Keeping your dog at his proper weight is not always easy. Corgis rapidly become obese, which is extremely detrimental to their general health. Your dog should have enough flesh to cover his bones, but it should be hard and not flabby. Check the standard in the first chapter for weight guidelines.

TYPES OF FOODS/TREATS

There are three types of commercially available dog food—dry, canned and semi-moist—and a huge assortment of treats (lucky dogs) to feed your dog. Which should you choose?

Dry and canned foods contain similar ingredients. The primary difference between them is their moisture content. The moisture is not just water; it's blood and broth, too, the very things that dogs adore. So while canned food is more palatable, dry food is more economical, convenient and effective in controlling tartar buildup. Most owners feed a 25% canned/75% dry diet to give their dogs the benefit of both. Just be sure your dog is getting the nutrition he needs (you and your veterinarian can determine this).

Semi-moist food has the flavor dogs love and the convenience owners want. However, they tend to contain excessive amounts of artificial colors and preservatives.

Dog treats come in every size, shape and flavor imaginable, from organic cookies shaped like postmen to beefy chew sticks. Dogs seem to love them all, so enjoy the variety. Just be sure not to overindulge your dog. Factor treats into his regular meal sizes.

Time for a Diet!

Any Corgi over 32 pounds, no matter how large his structure may be, is fat. Accustom your eyes to the right look, and be hard-hearted when he agitates for more tidbits. Generally speaking, females need to consume less than males to maintain the optimum weight. Of course, the amount of exercise he gets and the quality of the ingredients in his dinner are factors involved in the perfect equation. Watch him and adjust accordingly. If things get out of control, talk to your veterinarian, who can prescribe a scientifically formulated diet to promote weight loss.

Picky Eaters

There is a flip side to this coin—the picky eater. Every now and then a youngster will look at you as if to say, "You expect me to eat *this*?" Everything you put down will be eaten begrudgingly or not at all. This is not the result of illness, it is just picky eating.

Nevertheless, even a picky puppy is generally wolfing it down by the time he is 15 months old. In the meantime, select a flavor the puppy likes best, add raw meat or chicken, gravy or broth and offer small portions. Parmesan cheese sprinkled on top is a yummy enticement. Leave the food in the puppy's usual dining place for 10 to 15 minutes. Do not let anyone disturb or distract him. Pretend you are not watching. If he eats it, calmly tell him he is a good boy. If not, nonchalantly remove the remains, and do not feed him again until his next scheduled meal. He is not going to starve to death, but if he gets an obvious reaction out of you, he is going to perpetuate the behavior.

Foods to Avoid

Corgis are, for the most part, omnivores. But there are a few items that, tempting as they may be, are *truly* bad for them. Heading the list is chocolate; keep it out of reach. Chocolate contains theobromine, which can be deadly if eaten in large quantities. Onions are also bad for dogs, although garlic is beneficial. Regular cows' milk causes diarrhea. (As an alternative, canned or powdered milk is fine and useful for baby puppies that are being weaned.) Turkey skin will invariably upset the stomach, as will spicy salsa. Do not overdo the table scraps as they will unbalance the diet and may encourage the dog to believe that anything less succulent is beneath him. If you want to deter begging, *never* slip a scrap to him under the dining room table. Begging is a vice that is easy to learn but hard to eliminate.

To reiterate, any bones other than thick, hard marrow bones are dangerous. Poultry, lamb and pork bones splinter and get stuck in the throat or intestines. Beef rib or steak bones are not much safer, and fish bones should be avoided at all costs. Refrain to prevent pain and injury.

Pack a Lunch

Should you be off somewhere for the day or taking your dog with you on vacation, be sure to plan ahead for his needs. Bring along his own bowl and enough of his regular food for the duration. It may be hard to find your brand when you are far from home, and changing diets abruptly may lead to diarrhea. When traveling, do your best to keep him on the diet to which he is accustomed. Dogs always do best when their diet does not vary. Familiar food is easier on the dog's stomach, and provides one of the comforts of home.

Unfamiliar water contains different microbes than his tummy is accustomed to, so fill up a gallon jug of home water to bring along, too. If that runs out, buy bottled water and gradually introduce the local water.

chapter 6

Grooming Your Pembroke Welsh Corgi

The Welsh farmers of Pembrokeshire had no time to spend on the appearance of their all-purpose little helpers. An occasional bath when it was obviously necessary or maybe a quick swipe with a brush after returning from a muddy pasture was all these Corgis could expect. Fortunately, because their coats naturally repelled dirt

when it dried, they kept themselves fairly clean. Corgi owners today are grateful for this legacy. Corgis are easy to groom.

Today, however, there is nothing more scruffy and sad looking than a Corgi with a coat that is tufting out and ragged. No Corgi appearing in public should embarrass herself and the breed with a motley looking coat. Show pride in the breed you love. Keep your dog combed!

Basic Combing and Brushing

. . . WHEN

Although your dog will not have to be groomed each day to keep her coat from matting or snarling, there are many benefits to setting aside some time for her needs at least once a week. Corgis do shed, and dead hair can accumulate in their coats. If it is combed out regularly, the chore is a simple one. If neglected, it may take quite a bit of time and some discomfort for your dog before the comb slips through easily once again.

During the weekly session, her skin can be checked for sore spots, cuts and parasites. If you live in an area where fleas and ticks proliferate, it would be wise to give your dog a good once-over as often as possible, certainly after each walk in the woods. (These annoying pests are discussed in the next chapter.)

If grooming is a weekly routine, it should be a hassle-free event. Your dog will know what to expect, and more importantly, she will have learned to be handled and held without fussing. Young dogs need to be trained to accept this form of restraint. Besides, regular grooming provides a bonding time between person and dog, which is usually enjoyed by both.

. . . WHERE

On a Table

Many people groom their Corgis on a sturdy grooming table that has a nonslip top surface. These handy items may be purchased through pet supply catalogs or at dog shows, or they can be a handyman's project. Working at a table is more comfortable for the owner than bending down. However, any dog on a table must be watched constantly to prevent a fall or ill-fated jump. An added advantage of using a table is to accustom the dog to being off the ground. (She will be judged on a table at a dog show, which can be scary if she is not used to it.)

On the Floor

It's just as satisfactory—and perhaps more comforting—to sit with your dog on the floor for her grooming session. Set out a towel, position yourself on one end and let her settle down between your outspread legs with her head toward your feet. Have your grooming tools at hand along with a wastebasket or bag to catch the combings. You will need a steel comb with wide- and thin-spaced teeth, a fine-toothed flea comb and, optionally, a natural bristle brush. During the winter, using a spray bottle of water helps control static.

. . . How

Start with the wide-spaced side of the comb. Work from the top of the neck down the back and over the sides following the natural lay of the hair. Take fairly short, deep strokes but be careful that the skin is not scratched. Continue combing until the comb goes through the hair easily. It often takes a bit of a tug over the rump. Repeat with the finer spaced half of the comb. Gently place your

If the undercoat is quite thick, you may want to begin combing at the back.

dog on her side. Shift back to the wide teeth and start at the shoulder. Always comb the hair in the direction in which it grows. When combing the sides, it is easiest to do small sections from the thinner belly hair up to the top. Again,

repeat with the narrow teeth. Do not forget the legs, tummy and pants. Turn your dog over and do the other side. Lastly, comb the ruff. Fluff up with the brush.

Another way to work through the coat, especially if the undercoat is very thick, is to start at the back. Hold a section of hair back with one hand and little by little comb the lowest layer straight out. This works particularly well for the pants. Slowly work forward.

Combing for Fleas and Ticks

The flea comb is used to catch fleas and ticks. If the coat has not been prepared as described above, it is very hard to get a flea comb through it. Once a flea is trapped in the comb, kill it by squeezing it against your thumbnail or submerge it in a cup of water.

A well-groomed dog looks good and feels good.

Ticks should be pulled off with tweezers, being careful to get the head and put it in a scrap of paper, squashed or flushed. Do not touch them with your fingers as they could be carrying disease. There are dandy tick pickers on the market. It is possible to keep a Corgi flea- and tick-free, even at the buggiest time of year, by diligent combing as opposed to applying chemical sprays. It takes time, though, and just once a week will not suffice. (Managing fleas and removing ticks is discussed in detail in Chapter 7.)

Shedding

Your dog will need special attention when she is "throwing her coat." This thorough "molt" is triggered in bitches by hormone changes associated with their seasons or maternal duties. The hair comes out in handfuls. A mom who has just given birth is so naked there is nothing to do but laugh. The boys and spayed bitches go "out of coat" also, but not as often as intact females. Whenever you notice that the coat looks dry and little tufts of loose undercoat stick out on the shoulders or haunches, beware—it's going to be a hairy few weeks. Now is the time to comb your dog well every day or two. Pull out any loose clumps as they appear. When the old coat is almost gone, a warm bath hastens the rest of the molt. The guard hairs along the spine are the last to go. As funny as your dog looks now, within three weeks she will be clothed in beautiful shiny new fur! It is all part of being a Corgi.

Managing a Fluffy

A Corgi with a fluffy coat of lengthy, silky hair requires more grooming than a standard-coated one. This type of hair does not shed dirt readily, it collects grass, twigs and burrs, and will mat easily. A brush is useful to start the grooming process. Work from the back forward and bottom up, holding the hair up and smoothing one layer at a time. Watch out for mats, particularly behind the ears and under the forearms. Mats pull the skin and hurt when brushed, or when the dog moves. It may be necessary to cut them out. Combing a neglected fluffy can be quite a project and may take more than one session. If it becomes too much for you, take the dog to a groomer. A little judicious scissoring here and there may help, but do not let anyone shave her.

For either length of coat, but particularly with fluffies, it is important to check the anus on a regular basis. Perhaps it is the lack of tail, but certainly the profuse hair traps small pieces of fecal matter close to the skin. This can only be intensely irritating. A damp paper towel or brief spray in the sink will solve the problem. A dab of ointment will soothe any abrasion.

Other Weekly Chores

Grooming your dog isn't only a way to keep her looking healthy, it's also a time during which you can make sure she actually *is* healthy. Your dog's grooming session is a perfect time to check her eyes, ears and teeth.

KEEPING THE EYES CLEAN

Use a cotton ball to wipe away any excess tearing below the eye. If it is extensive or the eye is inflamed, contact your veterinarian, who can prescribe medication and prevent more serious eye problems from developing. If the dog is squinting, seek help at once.

CHECKING THE EARS

Corgis do not seem to have the ear problems that plague many other breeds. At grooming time, wipe out any dirt or wax from the outer part of the ear. Never put a cotton swab down the ear canal. If there is a crusty brown discharge or the ear emits an unpleasant odor, see your veterinarian.

DENTAL CHECK

Because doggy dental disease is a common misfortune, keep a weekly watch of your dog's mouth. Bad breath, decay, loss of teeth and periodontitis are widespread in the canine community. A little attention to the teeth at grooming time will go a long way to stave off these unpleasantries.

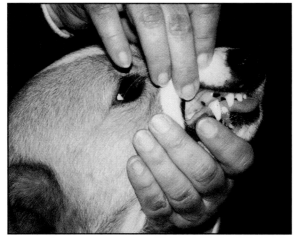

Check your dog's teeth and gums often. Dental hygiene is important to your dog's health.

Right from the start, get your dog accustomed to having her teeth cleaned. Take a piece of gauze or terry cloth with a bit of baking soda on it and wipe the plaque off her teeth. Doggy toothbrushes and toothpaste are for sale at pet supply stores. Do not use toothpaste designed for humans. Should calculus build up, particularly on the large back teeth, dental scalers for dogs can effectively remove it. To avoid nicking the gums, scale away from them down the teeth. Eventually, most dogs will need a professional cleaning under anesthesia.

Nail Detail

Many owners are put off by the thought of trimming a dog's nails. A pink quick runs down the nail which, if cut, can bleed and hurt. Fortunately, most Corgis have white paws with white nails, so the quick is visible in a good light and can be avoided. If your dog's footfall is clicking across the floor, it is time to trim the nails. Neglecting the nails will cause the feet to splay, affect her gait and eventually cause lameness should they grow so long they curl back into her pads. Ideally, the nails should clear the floor when the dog is standing. To keep them this way means trimming at least every two weeks unless they are worn down naturally by padding along city streets.

It is not hard to learn how to safely trim your dog's nails. A guillotine-type nail trimming tool is preferred by most people. The blade slides up when you close the handle. Be sure you work in good light. Until you get the hang of it, snip off only the hooks at the end of the nail. Cut across the top half of the nail only, not the entire nail. Be very careful. If you cut too much and draw blood, a styptic powder or even a bar of soap will take care of it. You probably will have to put your arm around the dog to steady her, but apply only as much pressure as is needed to keep her still. Corgis are more frightened by being held tight than by the clipping process itself. Reassure your dog that she is a good girl. Do only a little at a time if she is unhappy, but do not let her decide when you are going to stop. Give her a good hug when you are finished.

TAPING EARS

Many Corgi puppies leave for their new homes before their ears have become fully erect. Sometimes an ear that has been up will drop during teething time. If this happens, the ear needs to be taped into an upright position for a few days. Take a 6-inch strip of 1-inch-wide masking or adhesive tape and with someone holding the puppy, start at the base of the ear in the back. Wrap the tape around the ear to the front. (The objective is to support the ear where it folds over.) Use only enough tape to do the trick. Gently release any hairs that might irritate the puppy by being caught in the edge of the tape. Leave the ears taped for a few days. Repeat as necessary, giving the ear a rest between tapings. If this procedure does not work in due time, ask your breeder or veterinarian to help you.

A good way to trim nails is to sit on the floor with your dog on her back steadied with your knees. Work from the underside of the nail and start the blade near the tip. Again, hold her only as tightly as necessary, pat her calmly and do not tense up yourself. If there is a struggle, rest until she quiets down and then continue. Do not accept bad behavior or give up on her terms. When you are done hold her in your arms and pat her until she relaxes and is soaking up the affection. With this approach, your dog will soon be quite comfortable with nail trimming and might even volunteer.

Many dog owners prefer to grind the nails with a high speed, handheld electric tool. These can be purchased at a hardware store or through a dog supply catalog. They are light, small and can be cordless. Look for at least 25,000 rpm (revolutions per minute) as the top speed. The beauty of using a grinder is that you have tremendous

A guillotine-type trimmer is a very popular tool for nail trimming.

control and can shorten the nail back to the quick without drawing any blood. Dogs definitely prefer the grinder over other trimming devices (once they become accustomed to the sound). Stroke the nail lightly and shift from nail to nail after just a few passes to avoid heat buildup from the friction. If you have not trimmed the nails for a few weeks, a combination of clipping the tips and grinding the rest will save time.

While trimming nails, every so often trim the hair on your dog's feet. Remove the growth under the pads and neaten up the edges of the sides, but do not cut the hair too high. Older or infirm dogs benefit from the improved traction of trimmed feet, especially on slippery floors. Neat feet look classy.

Bath Time

It's not necessary to give your dog frequent baths. With adequate grooming, she will keep herself clean for quite a while. If her bedding is laundered and she is toweled off on rainy days, she won't acquire a "doggy odor." However, a healthy sudsing will freshen the skin and sparkle the coat. Select a shampoo that is formulated for dogs. Do not shampoo your dog with products designed for humans. As washing removes the natural oils in the coat, the hair will not lie flat for a few days. Keep this in mind, should you be planning to take your dog to a dog show. Give the bath several days in advance.

Gather several absorbent towels, a washcloth, a comb, a hair dryer and the shampoo in preparation for your dog's bath. In the typical household you have a choice of the bathtub, the kitchen sink or a set tub to wash the little Corgi in. It is a matter of preference. A spray hose attachment is a decided advantage.

WASHING YOUR DOG

Let your dog go out to relieve herself while you get the water warmed up. Put her in the tub/sink. Some people advocate putting cotton balls in the ears, but this is not really necessary if you are reasonably careful, and it may be annoying to the dog. Start by wetting your dog all over except for the head. With the shampoo, lather up a ring around the neck. This prevents any resident fleas (horrors) from rushing onto her head. Work shampoo into the back, down the sides and on her chest and tummy. Pick up each leg and wash it. Be sure to clean her down to the skin. With a damp cloth, wipe out the insides of the ears. The face can be carefully washed, but take care around the eyes. Soap stings dogs, too.

RINSE AND DRY

Once the washing is completed, thoroughly rinse your dog with lots of fresh water. It is critical to remove all the soap to prevent itchy skin and may take quite a while. A second soaping usually is not necessary.

Next, using at least two towels, dry her as best you can, then carry her to a spot where you can plug in the hair dryer. Puppies often are frightened by the dryer, but older dogs learn to enjoy the warmth. Blow-dry the back first and then the tummy. With the comb, separate the hair clumps. The areas over the hocks and behind the ears dry slowly, and a thick ruff is the last to dry. Do not forget to dry the legs and feet. With the combination of the comb and the dryer, your dog will soon be gorgeous and squeaky clean (if a bit fuzzy for a few days). The short time a bath takes will have been well spent.

GROOMING TOOLS

Steel comb with fine- and medium-spaced teeth

Fine-toothed flea comb

Natural bristle brush

Guillotine-style nail clipper and/ or electric nail grinder

pH balanced shampoo

Tooth-cleaning equipment

Dog towels

Keeping Your Pembroke Welsh Corgi Healthy

The Pembrokes that we know today are not significantly different from the sturdy fellows that were going about their chores in the demanding environment of the Welsh homesteads centuries ago. They were a hardy lot then, and they are now. Few breed-specific health problems affect Corgis. Barring mishap and with reasonable care, a Corgi's average lifespan is from 13 to 15 years. To ensure that your Corgi will enjoy good health throughout his life, you must learn to be conscientious about his basic medical needs and alert to any sign which may forebode trouble.

Selecting a Veterinarian

First on the list is the selection of a competent veterinarian. Your veterinarian should be well-educated, knowledgeable and up-to-date.

The office will ideally be within 30 minutes travel, perfectly clean and covered during off-hours by some sort of emergency service or clinic. If there is more than one veterinarian with the practice, you and your dog can be seen without undue delay even during vacation months. Moreover, co-evaluation might be invaluable in case of a difficult diagnosis.

IDENTIFYING YOUR DOG

It's a terrible thing to think about, but your dog could somehow, someday, get lost or stolen. How would you get him back? Your best bet would be to have some form of identification on your dog. You can choose from a collar and tags, a tattoo, a microchip or a combination of these three.

Every dog should wear a buckle collar with identification tags. They are the quickest and easiest way for a stranger to identify your dog. It's best to inscribe the tags with your name and phone number; you don't need to include your dog's name.

There are two ways to permanently identify your dog. The first is a tattoo, placed on the inside of your dog's thigh. The tattoo should be your dog's AKC registration number.

The second is a microchip, a rice-sized pellet that's inserted under the dog's skin at the base of the neck, between the shoulder blades. When a scanner is passed over the dog, it will beep, notifying the person that the dog has a chip. The scanner will then show a code, identifying the dog. Microchips are becoming more and more popular and are certainly the wave of the future.

The most important factor in your selection is the confidence that your Corgi will be treated with care and consideration, evinced in the veterinarian's ongoing love for the work he does and the animals he treats. Corgis quickly size up an indifferent or hostile veterinarian. Avoid one who routinely ties the dogs by the neck to the examining table. Corgis do not care for this and become frightened and uncooperative.

Most veterinarians practice traditional medicine. There is a growing number, however, who also include holistic disciplines such as acupuncture, homeopathy, nutritional analysis and vitamin-mineral-glandular supplements. The object is to balance the body in general and support its ability to promote healing from within, as opposed to primarily focusing on a symptom. Alternative treatments have been known to be very effective for some ailing dogs. Obviously, you must feel comfortable with your veterinarian and his methods.

If you are new in town, ask for a recommendation from a friend who takes his dog's welfare seriously. Do not hesitate to call the office and ask questions about the facilities and the veterinarian. You could even drop by and get a feel for the place yourself. Having just the right veterinarian will make a great deal of difference to your peace of mind—and your Corgi's well-being. An open line of communication is essential. You should feel comfortable calling with a problem or with a question about ongoing treatment.

Vaccinations

All veterinarians offer modern vaccinations against a multitude of canine diseases. The recommended frequency and variety of these shots varies from practice to practice. Puppies are routinely given several doses of vaccine, spaced from 8 to 16 weeks of age, to protect them while the immunity they received from their dam gradually wears off and ceases to conflict with the immunity induced by the inoculations. Annual revaccination is accepted protocol. Certain vaccinations, described below, are highly advisable, but the vaccination for rabies is mandatory. Other immunizations are optional and perhaps even questionable. As it is quite possible to make a Corgi ill by pumping too many things into his little body, discuss your concerns with your veterinarian and use discretion. Less is definitely better than more.

WHEN TO CALL THE VET

In any emergency situation, you should call your veterinarian immediately. You can make the difference in your dog's life by staying as calm as possible when you call and by giving the doctor or the assistant as much information as possible before you leave for the clinic. That way, the vet will be able to take immediate, specific action to remedy your dog's situation.

Emergencies include acute abdominal pain, suspected poisoning, snakebite, burns, frostbite, shock, dehydration, abnormal vomiting or bleeding, and deep wounds. You are the best judge of your dog's health, as you live with and observe him every day. Don't hesitate to call your veterinarian if you suspect trouble.

Major Diseases

The major diseases against which the common DHLPP vaccine provide protection are:

Distemper   Distemper is an extremely contagious viral disease that has decimated the canine population in its past. Whole kennels were wiped out, and puppies fared the worst. The disease is now under control, as a result of widespread immunization.

73

Symptoms of distemper include lethargy, fever and a runny nose and eyes, coughing, vomiting and diarrhea. In the advanced stages, brain damage is likely.

Infectious Canine Hepatitis This virus is also highly contagious and potentially lethal. It is communicable only from dog to dog and affects the liver, kidneys and blood vessels. The virus is shed in the urine, feces and saliva of ill dogs. Symptoms range from depression and loss of appetite to a high fever accompanied by bloody diarrhea and vomiting. Jaundice and a sensitivity to light are additional symptoms. A recovering dog may have a characteristic clouding of the eye.

Leptospirosis Leptospirosis is caused by a bacteria that enters the dog's system through a break in the skin or via ingestion of water that has been contaminated by the urine of an affected animal. Most cases are mild or subclinical, and dogs often develop natural antibodies against it. However, leptopirosis can cause serious kidney and liver damage. In areas where the disease is prevalent, more frequent vaccination is suggested.

Parvovirus Parvo, as it is called, made headlines in the 1970s. It caused chaos with entire litters of puppies succumbing to an odd smelling form of bloody diarrhea. Older dogs were sickened as well. It was later discovered that the hearts of many of the survivors had been impaired. This super-contagious disease is transmitted through the feces of an affected dog. Just a bite on the postman's shoe could carry it from door to door. Dog shows, always a source of contagion, became a hazard. Concerned exhibitors wiped off their dogs' feet and their own shoes with a disinfecting solution of household bleach. This practice continues as a safeguard against parvo.

> ## YOUR PUPPY'S VACCINES
>
> Vaccines are given to prevent your dog from getting an infectious disease like canine distemper or rabies. Vaccines are the ultimate preventive medicine: they're given before your dog ever gets the disease so as to protect him from the disease. That's why it is necessary for your dog to be vaccinated routinely. Puppy vaccines start at 8 weeks of age for the five-in-one DHLPP vaccine and are given every three to four weeks until the puppy is 16 months old. Your veterinarian will put your puppy on a proper schedule and will remind you when to bring in your dog for shots.

The coronavirus, related to parvo, similarly causes runny yellow stools, but is much milder and seldom fatal to adult dogs.

Parainfluenza (Kennel Cough) This respiratory, air-borne, viral-induced disease spreads rapidly wherever dogs gather. Several viruses are involved, and new strains frequently appear. Boarding kennel owners insist that their clients have current vaccinations against kennel cough before they are admitted. Nonetheless, often the boarders return home and in a few days are coughing away. Treatment usually consists of a cough suppressant, and the problem clears up by itself. However, if secondary bacteria invades the lungs, chronic bronchitis can result.

Rabies The vaccine against rabies, a virus found in the saliva of an affected animal, is not included with the usual multiple shot described above. In fact, it should not be given at the same time as the DHLPP shot to avoid overloading the dog's system. After the initial one-year dose, authoritative veterinarians recommend shifting to a dose given once every three years. This is one immunization that must be kept in force.

Keeping your dog's vaccinations up-to-date will help him live a longer, happier life.

Rabies is a devastating, deadly disease spread from affected wildlife to dogs, cats and humans. In many areas, it is on the rise. Bats, skunks and raccoons frequently become rabid. Beware of any wild animals that are acting strangely.

There is another good reason to keep your Corgi's rabies shots up-to-date. Should he inadvertently bite someone, he will not be quarantined or even destroyed by the authorities, if you can provide proof of this vaccination which is required by law.

Internal Parasites

Many parasitic worms and other organisms reside inside the body of the dog. They can involve the gastrointestinal tract, the heart, the lungs, and even the bladder. If allowed to proliferate, they can cause severe illness or death. Your veterinarian can identify and treat these parasites effectively. A fecal or blood sample examined under a microscope can reveal the presence of internal parasites.

Roundworms   These 4-inch-long white worms look disgustingly like vermicelli. Almost all puppies are

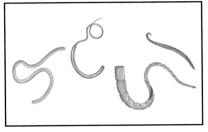

Common internal parasites (l-r): roundworm, whipworm, tapeworm and hookworm.

born with roundworms, as the larvae can be encapsulated in the dam's flesh, reactivated during pregnancy and travel through the placenta into the fetus. The roundworm may lay 200,000 eggs a day, which are passed in the feces. Puppy and adult alike can easily become infected from contaminated soil. It is important to pick up your dog's stool daily as a measure to control any kind of worms. When walking your dog in public areas beware of what others leave behind.

The signs of a wormy puppy are a dry, lackluster coat, a potbelly and a thin neck. Sometimes the baby will cough up a worm, or one may appear in watery stools. Little puppies need to be treated with a safe wormer several times to catch the worms before they mature and start shedding eggs. After the puppy has gone to his new home, veterinary treatment for roundworm should continue as long as required to clear the problem.

Hookworms   Only ¼- to ½-inch long, hookworms latch onto the wall of the small intestines and suck blood. Puppies can also acquire hookworms from the dam in utero, and once again infection arises from eggs passed in the feces. Chronic infestation causes bloody diarrhea, anemia and weight loss. Most medications which control roundworms will catch hookworms as well. Your veterinarian can advise you after a fecal exam what medicine will be most effective.

Whipworms   Adult whipworms are 2 to 3 inches long with a thick and thin appearance (resembling a whip), although you are not likely to see them. They reside in the large intestines, and because they lay few eggs, their presence is harder to detect via a stool sample. It may take more than one check to come up with a diagnosis. Diarrhea, an unhealthy look and weight loss are signs of whipworm infection. As with other intestinal parasites, whipworm eggs contaminate the soil.

Tapeworms   Tapeworms are a flat, segmented worm that can grow to several feet. However, they are usually detected when ¼-inch segments break off and appear around the dog's rectum. Fresh, moist pieces wiggle, and dried ones look just like uncooked rice. Fleas are an intermediary host for tapeworms. If a dog swallows a flea, chances are he will eventually develop tapeworms. The veterinarian can give an effective medication that will kill the worm in one application. Unfortunately, if fleas continue to flourish, the dog can become reinfested with tapeworms, too. Dogs with tapeworms do not look sick.

Heartworms   These insidious creatures are the most dangerous of all internal parasites. As their name implies, the long, thin adult worms lodge in the heart, and if untreated they will eventually compromise its function. They, too, are transmitted by an intermediary host, the mosquito. In warm, moist areas of the country where these insects abide year-round, heartworm infection is most prevalent.

Prevention is far easier than the cure. If no microfilaria (larval worms) appear in a blood sample, the dog can be put on a daily or monthly heartworm preventative. In regions where incidence is low, some veterinarians prefer to test the dog twice a year rather than subject him to daily doses of what is, in fact, a poison. Caught in the early stages, heartworms can be eradicated with relative safety. Let your veterinarian advise you, but be aware that some Corgis have had nasty reactions to the monthly heartworm pill, especially when given at the same time as a set of vaccinations.

Giardia   Giardia is a protozoan, not a worm, but it has the same effect as a worm, causing diarrhea tinged with blood and general poor health. It is commonly associated with water contamination and poor kennel situations where the pens are not thoroughly sanitized. Puppies are particularly susceptible to contracting giardia. Identification of the problem is through a microscopic fecal examination, and a short course of the appropriate medication will eradicate the infection.

External Parasites

You should be aware of external parasites that live on your dog's skin. These include fleas, ticks and mange mites.

The flea is a die-hard pest.

Fleas   The adult flea is a small, brown insect about ⅛ of an inch long. It can easily be seen hurrying along

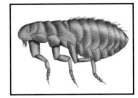

through your dog's fur. Fleas cannot fly, but they sure can jump and are amazingly evasive. Even if you do not catch a glimpse of a flea, you can tell just by looking that they are living on your dog when you find tiny specks of black dirt on the skin. This is dried blood excreted by these bloodsucking insects. When a wet tissue is applied to these dots, it will turn red.

Not surprisingly, you can suspect fleas if your dog quickly turns to bite an itchy spot, or worse, if he is scratching away furiously. Many Corgis have only a mild reaction to fleas. Others are hypersensitive to flea saliva and suffer greatly from severe skin reactions and the resultant hot spots. Fleas are not only a nuisance—a severe infestation can result in anemia due to blood loss, as they transmit tapeworms.

Getting rid of fleas is a challenge. Effective flea control requires treating the environment as well as the dog. The dog can be washed and/or combed free of the critters, but he will not stay that way if fleas are hanging around the house, yard and car. There are numerous chemical and natural botanical weapons to help in the battle. Some are more toxic than others. If you use them, read the labels carefully and follow the instructions.

In addition to collars, sprays, bombs, shampoos and dips, it is possible to apply a drop of a special chemical on the skin which will act systemically to repel and kill fleas. The procedure works well enough, but who is to guarantee its safety for a chemical-sensitive Corgi? Another option is a natural product, diatomaceous earth, which acts mechanically on insects by destroying their ectoskeleton and causes them to dehydrate. Again, follow the recommendations.

If the flea population is minimal, vacuum the house thoroughly in every cranny, wash the bedding and keep combing the bathed Corgi as described in the chapter on grooming. Be grateful that the Corgi is a small dog with hair readily penetrated by a comb.

FIGHTING FLEAS

Remember, the fleas you see on your dog are only part of the problem—the smallest part! To rid your dog and home of fleas, you need to treat your dog *and* your home. Here's how:

• Identify where your pet(s) sleep. These are "hot spots."

• Clean your pets' bedding regularly by vacuuming and washing.

• Spray "hot spots" with a non-toxic, long-lasting flea larvicide.

• Treat outdoor "hot spots" with insecticide.

• Kill eggs on pets with a product containing insect growth regulators (IGRs).

• Kill fleas on pets per your veterinarian's recommendation.

Ticks   The ticks that most commonly attach themselves to dogs are the brown dog tick and the deer tick. The former is, as an adult, about the size of a flat match head. The engorged females look like a gray raisin. Deer ticks, on the other hand, are extremely small, dark brown walking dots. They remain quite small even when engorged. In their larval stage, they are minute. (Look for them on the eyelids, especially in the spring.) Ticks are dangerous not only because their bites can leave sores but because of the diseases they

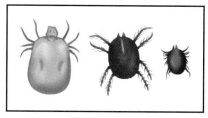

Three types of ticks (l-r): the wood tick, brown dog tick and deer tick.

79

might be carrying. Rocky Mountain Spotted Fever and the infamous Lyme Disease, among others, are transmitted by ticks.

It is important to keep a close watch for ticks and remove them as soon as possible, preferably before they have had time to swell. Some people advocate stunning the tick first with alcohol, petroleum jelly or insecticide. Do not use a match (for obvious reasons).

With tweezers or a tick picker, grasp the tick close to the skin and try to pull the head out with the body. A little antiseptic ointment will heal the bite. Avoid squeezing the tick, as its body fluids might contain disease-carrying microbes, which will then be injected into the host animal.

Other Parasites There are assorted microscopic spider-like creatures that cause different kinds of skin problems including sarcoptic and demodectic mange. Should your dog show scaly, bare patches of skin that become red and itchy, by all means whisk him to the veterinarian,

Use tweezers to remove ticks from your dog.

who can make a diagnosis through a skin scraping. (This is one for the pros.) The sarcoptic variety is treatable, but demodectic mange can be very difficult to control.

General Care

In addition to maintaining a vaccination schedule and parasite control under the guidance of your veterinarian, routine health care for your Corgi is easy. In an earlier chapter, attention to the eyes, ears, teeth and nails were discussed as part of the routine grooming session. Good nutrition, clean water, plenty of exercise, sunlight, fresh air . . . it is the standard prescription for vibrant health. Corgis are seldom bothered by anything more than an occasional tummy upset due to dietary indiscretion or a passing "bug" or perhaps by a "sports" injury. Just keep an eye open to your dog's general demeanor. He will undoubtedly let you know if something is amiss.

INDICATIONS OF POSSIBLE HEALTH PROBLEMS

As healthy as they are as a breed, there are a few medical conditions that occur with enough frequency in Pembroke Welsh Corgis to warrant mention.

Back Trouble

In the back, the separate vertebrae in the spine are cushioned from each other by a spongy disc. If the disc ruptures, the interior material extrudes and presses against the spinal cord causing pain and/or paralysis of the hind limbs. Treatment depends upon the severity of the problem. Minor cases can be completely healed with crate rest and anti-inflammatory medication or very successfully with acupuncture.

The more rare, severe case might respond to surgery aimed at relieving pressure on the cord. Early signs of disc trouble include a reluctance to stand up or to climb stairs and a head-down posture. As the disability progresses, lack of coordination will become apparent. Any Corgi exhibiting these signs should be examined by a veterinarian and have his activities totally restricted—leash walk only.

Run your hands regularly over your dog to feel for any injuries.

People used to think that disc trouble was the result of having a long back. While it is true that Dachshunds are plagued with disc disease, several other long, low breeds are not. Many square shaped breeds do suffer a high incidence of the problem. A Corgi need not curtail normal activities in order to prevent back trouble, although jumping off high places is not recommended for any dog. If a disc is going to rupture, it could happen by just turning over in bed.

Urinary Tract Infections

Some Corgis are inclined to develop urinary tract disorders such as cystitis or bladder stones. Frequent and painful urination, blood in the urine or the excretion of small gravelly matter are telltale signs. The veterinarian can provide relief with an appropriate antibiotic and a urine acidifier. In the case of stones, a special prescription diet fed exclusively for a month or so has been found to dissolve certain types of these aggregations. Other cases require surgical removal.

Conscientious breeders work to eliminate genetic diseases from the gene pool, resulting in healthy puppies.

GENETIC DISEASES AND GENETIC SCREENING

There are three diseases of genetic origin found in Corgis: hip dysplasia, eye abnormalities and von Willebrand's Disease. Conscientious breeders are working to eliminate these diseases from the gene pool through premating diagnostic tests.

Hip Dysplasia

Hip dysplasia occurs when the head of the femur (leg bone) does not fit snugly into the hip socket, and the bones are worn down due to play in the motion of the leg. It can be painful and lead to obvious lameness. Hip dysplasia is caused by a number of factors including environmental influences during puppyhood and an inherited predisposition. The condition of the hip joint can be revealed by specially taken x-rays and other procedures that measure the relative luxation of the femur. The Orthopedic Foundation for Animals (OFA) is an organization that reads x-rays of dogs over 2 years old and assigns a grade ranging from clear to severely dysplastic. Those dogs passing the OFA's requirements for certification are recommended for breeding.

Unfortunately, breeding out hip dysplasia is not very easy. Dysplastic puppies appear in litters with two clear parents, and mildly dysplastic parents can produce clear puppies. Still, it is well worthwhile to try every avenue open to eliminate this debilitating disease. Hip dysplasia is common in many of the large breeds. Although the disease can appear in the Pembroke Welsh Corgi, because of the breed's unique structure they fortunately seldom become lame. Dogs with radiographically diagnosed hip dysplasia have won well or have had major wins at dog shows where exemplary movement is rewarded.

Genetic Eye Disorders

Eye abnormalities include Progressive Retinal Atrophy (PRA), juvenile cataracts, persistent pupillary membranes (PPM) and retinal folds. The worst of these, PRA, which causes total blindness at an early age in many breeds, is almost nonexistent in Pembroke Corgis. The other three abnormalities are not disastrous and seldom cause sight impairment. Nonetheless, as these problems are of genetic origin, it is wise to test for them. The Canine Eye Registration Foundation (CERF) certifies dogs examined by members of the American College of Veterinary Opthamologists.

Von Willebrand's Disease

Von Willebrand's Disease, a bleeding disorder that prohibits clotting, was first recognized in Pembroke Welsh Corgis in the 1970s. Dogs that are genetically clear of the disease bred to other clear dogs produce only clear offspring. However, a dog may be a carrier of the gene causing von Willebrand's Disease and have no clinical symptoms. A carrier bred to a carrier can produce affected puppies. The worst scenario, obviously, is a dog that bleeds to death. Because of complicated genetics, however, the effects of the troublesome gene are not always expressed. Abnormal thyroid function seems to be involved in the equation as well. There is a blood test available that can determine whether a dog is likely to be clear of the gene or a carrier and/or affected. Once again, breeding stock should be tested. In addition, it is useful to know if your outwardly normal Corgi is subclinically affected, so support can be made available in advance of planned surgery.

It must be stressed that while these diseases do exist in the breed, and every effort should be made to purify the gene pool, the average Corgi will live his life without being bothered by them. Generally, the Corgi is a hardy, healthy little fellow.

Spaying and Neutering

One of the first things you should consider when you bring home a puppy is scheduling spay or neutering surgery. During the spaying procedure for females, the ovaries, tubes and uterus are removed. Males are neutered by the removal of their testicles. This routine surgery is usually done at about 6 months of age, before the sexual hormones develop. Bitches

---

ADVANTAGES OF SPAY/NEUTER

The greatest advantage of spaying (for females) or neutering (for males) your dog is that you are guaranteed your dog will not produce puppies. There are too many puppies already available for too few homes. There are other advantages as well.

ADVANTAGES OF SPAYING

No messy heats.

No "suitors" howling at your windows or waiting in your yard.

Decreased incidences of pyometra (disease of the uterus) and breast cancer.

ADVANTAGES OF NEUTERING

Lessens male aggressive and territorial behaviors, but doesn't affect the dog's personality. Behaviors are often owner-induced, so neutering is not the only answer, but it is a good start.

Prevents the need to roam in search of bitches in season.

Decreased incidences of urogenital diseases.

spayed before their first season have a significantly lower incidence of mammary tumors later in life than those that go through even one season or are never spayed. They do not go through the biannual heat season, which lasts about three weeks, and is messy and aggravating for all. The males are much less likely to exhibit territorial behaviors triggered by hormones such as wandering, marking (leg lifting) and dog-to-dog aggression. It is not true that altered animals become fat and lazy. Weight and condition is a function of diet and exercise which must be tailored to suit each individual's metabolic needs.

The only reasons not to alter your Corgi are if you plan to show in conformation or if you are going to breed your dog. Altered animals are eligible to compete in every phase of canine activity except the beauty shows, which historically were to showcase breeding stock. If you purchased your Corgi as a pet from a breeder, you were probably given a spay-neuter contract and/or a Limited Registration application form for the AKC. You will be obligated to proceed with the operation when the dog reaches a certain age. Few puppies are of such high quality that they are retained intact as show prospects or to perpetuate the breed.

As cute as puppies are, there are too many abandoned dogs in this country. It is far wiser to alter your dog.

Why to Not Breed

Many people contemplate breeding for the wrong reasons. "Our Corgi is such a wonderful dog. We want another just like him." You will never reproduce your dog. No Corgi is exactly like any other Corgi any more than two humans are exactly alike. If you are enamored with his qualities, the closest you could come is to find another puppy with the same parents or parents of similar bloodlines. Offering him at stud sounds dandy, but somebody else will do all the work of raising the litter, and what will the bitch contribute genetically to the union? Your dog will not suffer if he never has a chance to breed.

While it is truly fascinating and educational to watch puppies being born, with Corgis this is an anxious time and sometimes heartbreaking. Regretfully, all too often a Caesarean section is required in the middle of the night to save the exhausted dam and her babies. Newborns need constant attention and do not always survive. A great deal of time, effort and money goes into raising a litter of puppies properly. It certainly is no way to make a fast buck. Moreover, there is no merit in adding to dog overpopulation. There are never enough good homes to go around.

The fact that you have a purebred dog with papers is no guarantee of quality. If you are not interested in showing, you probably have a wonderful pet dog that may be good-looking and indeed is a marvelous companion. Enjoy and treasure him as such. Let the breeding stock be the top of the line dogs that have carefully planned pedigrees, come close to the standard and are tested and found to be free of genetic diseases.

When Your Corgi Seems Sick

Corgis, with their expressive faces and eloquent body language, are transparent when it comes to how they feel. It then becomes your job to figure out what is wrong. What are the symptoms? Here are some questions to ask yourself before phoning the veterinarian:

Vomiting   Digested food or undigested food that has been regurgitated before reaching the stomach? Any foreign matter or blood? Just yellow or white foam? For how long and how often has the dog been vomiting?

Stools Normal or diarrhea? Just loose or watery? Color? Mucus or blood? Odd smell? How frequent?

Fever A dog's normal temperature is between 101 and 102°F. Anything over 103° is cause for concern. Use a rectal thermometer lubricated with petroleum jelly, gently insert 1 inch into the rectum, and hold it there for about 3 minutes, remove, wipe and read. Digital thermometers also work well for dogs.

Signs of Pain Limping? Tummy tucked up? Shivering? Panting? Swelling? Lumps or bleeding?

General Spirits Lethargic? Not eating? Bloodshot, tearing eyes?

Make a list of your findings and any unusual circumstances before you call or see your veterinarian. All these observations will help to determine what is ailing your dog. Corgis are smart, but they cannot talk.

Emergencies and First Aid

There are times when you have to act at once, even before you can get needed emergency veterinary care. Perhaps you are not at home, or the clinic is closed and the covering emergency facility is far away. There are a few handy first aid techniques to have tucked in the back of your mind. But first, if at all possible, call your veterinarian or the emergency clinic. Know just where to find the telephone numbers so you do not have to scramble for them.

A FIRST-AID KIT

Keep a canine first-aid kit on hand for general care and emergencies. Check it periodically to make sure liquids haven't spilled or dried up, and replace medications and materials after they're used. Your kit should include:

Activated charcoal tablets

Adhesive tape
(1 and 2 inches wide)

Antibacterial ointment
(for skin and eyes)

Aspirin (buffered or enteric coated, *not* Ibuprofen)

Bandages: Gauze rolls (1 and 2 inches wide) and dressing pads

Cotton balls

Diarrhea medicine

Dosing syringe

Hydrogen peroxide (3%)

Petroleum jelly

Rectal thermometer

Rubber gloves

Rubbing alcohol

Scissors

Tourniquet

Towel

Tweezers

Personal Safety Measures

When a dog is frightened and in pain he may snap as you try to help him. If your Corgi is not used to your working on him, the safest thing to do is devise a temporary muzzle. Knot a piece of gauze or old stocking leg around the top of his muzzle, down under the chin and then behind the ears.

Measures to Be Taken

Use a scarf or old hose to make a temporary muzzle, as shown.

Occasionally, your dog will require first aid in order to prevent a situation from escalating while you transport him to the veterinarian. The following are some events that will require first aid and the appropriate measures that should be taken.

Animal Bites Puncture wounds inflicted on your dog by other animal's bites can easily become infected because the teeth carry bacteria into the flesh and sometimes the small opening heals over trapping the germs inside. (Cat bites are particularly dangerous.) Trim the hair away from the site and liberally rinse the wound with hydrogen peroxide. Pat it dry with a cotton ball and apply an antiseptic ointment. Keep the wound open until it heals from within. If swelling occurs, you may have to hot pack it for a few days.

If the wound is large, deep or a tear, a stitch may be in order. Place gauze or a clean cloth over the wound and apply pressure to control the bleeding. If a leg wound does not stop bleeding, you can try a tourniquet above the site as you transport the dog to the veterinarian as rapidly as possible. Release the tourniquet every 15 minutes.

Insect Stings Remove the stinger if possible with tweezers, apply a paste of baking soda to the site and watch carefully. Sometimes an allergic reaction sets in, and the eyelids and muzzle begin to swell. If you see these signs, call the veterinarian immediately. If the reaction is mild, he may suggest an antihistamine tablet or Benadryl. A severe reaction is life-threatening.

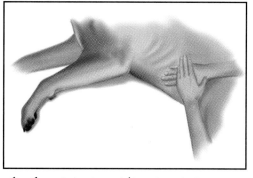

Choking If the dog is drooling, pawing his jaws or gasping, look into his mouth. You may need to use a flashlight. If you can see something blocking the throat, try to get it out at once with your fingers, tweezers or even pliers. If it does not budge or you cannot see anything, try hitting him on the back of the neck between the shoulders. Should this not dislodge the object, try a doggy Heimlich maneuver. Being careful not to damage the ribs, press sharply behind the ribs with the palms of your hands. This can be done with the dog either standing or lying on his side. If you cannot remove the object, rush to the veterinary clinic.

Applying abdominal thrusts can save a choking dog.

Heatstroke It's amazing how many dogs are left to perish in unventilated cars each summer. *Never* leave your Corgi in a car unattended, even with the windows cracked. Should he become overheated, have difficulty breathing, pant rapidly or begin to stagger, act at once. Get him into cool water or hose him down. Check his temperature and seek the help of a veterinarian.

Fractures and Other Traumas When a dog suffers a fracture or trauma, a muzzle is truly a necessity. The objective is to move the injured area as little as possible while transporting the dog to the veterinarian. If a leg appears to be broken, try to immobilize it using a short piece of wood, padded, and tied on with gauze or tape. A magazine or roll of newspaper will not do for a Corgi-sized leg. If there has been a car accident, devise a stretcher from a board or something to keep his body from bending and adding to the damage. If he is quite still and his gums are white, he probably is in shock. Hurry!

Poisoning   Dogs, especially puppies, eat all sorts of things that they shouldn't. Some poisonous items are listed in the chapter on bringing home a puppy. Warfarin, slug bait and antifreeze top the list of dangerous poisons. If you suspect that your dog has eaten poison, the first thing to do is find out what has been ingested. Then call your veterinarian or the National Animal Poison Control Center hotline (1-800-548-2434). Let the trained personnel tell you whether to induce vomiting and how to do so. In some types of poisoning, inducing vomiting is *not* appropriate. Do not second guess the proper response.

Some of the many household substances harmful to your dog.

There are many varied emergency situations that can happen to you and your dog. Chapter 12, "Recommended Reading," lists several excellent books on health care and first aid. The more you read, the better prepared you will be to help your Corgi friend in a time of need.

Administering Medicine
PILLS

To give a pill, open the mouth wide, then drop it in the back of the throat.

Chances are that at some point during his life, you will need to give your dog some medicine. The easiest way is to bury the pill or liquid in his food, but this does not always work out as planned. A sick dog may not want to eat anything at all, and Corgis are amazingly adept at picking around the pills. A "special treat" of a meatball or wad of cream cheese often will sneak a pill past his guard.

The time may come, however, when you have to know how to get a pill down your dog's throat. Have the dog sit somewhere where he cannot back up too rapidly. Place one hand over the top of his muzzle so the fingers can pry up his jaw. With the other hand push the lower jaw down, and with the thumb and forefinger quickly place the pill on the back of the tongue. Once it is in, close the mouth, hold the chin up and rub his throat until he swallows. Do not forget to praise him during and afterwards.

LIQUID MEDICATIONS

Occasionally, you may have to administer medications in liquid form to your dog. The following are instructions on the most effective way to do so.

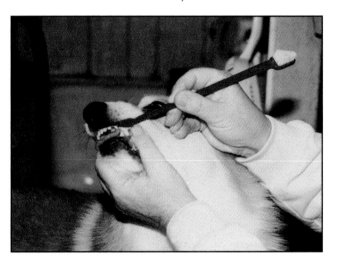

Keeping your dog's teeth clean is an essential part of helping him remain healthy.

Oral Medications

Administering liquids can be messy. A dropper is the best tool to do the trick, although a small spoon works once you get the hang of it. With the dog's head tilted up, grasp and pull out the corner of the mouth so there is a pocket between the cheek and the back teeth. Squirt or pour the liquid in the pocket and let it seep past the teeth and down the throat. Keep holding the head up until the medicine is swallowed.

*Squeeze eye
ointment into
the lower lid.*

Eye Ointments

To medicate the eyes, a line of ointment should be squeezed from the tube into a pocket made by holding down the lower lid with your thumb. Gently massage

the eyelids to spread the ointment. Eye drops need no special instructions. For skin lesions, be sure the ointment reaches through the hair down to the skin itself.

HEALING WOUNDS

If your Corgi should develop a condition that will not heal with his constant self-administrations, the veterinarian may require him to wear an Elizabethan collar so he cannot reach to lick or bite the wound. These lampshade devices extend beyond the nose and are held in place by a dog collar. At first he will be upset and miserable, but Corgis are usually good sports and soon lean to manage a bowl of food and other necessities. One fellow had great fun slinging gravel at a wall with his contraption. His owner always came to find out what the racket was and stayed to play.

*An Elizabethan
collar keeps
your dog from
licking a fresh
wound.*

Old Age

Gradually as time passes you will notice that your dog is aging. He may have white hairs on his face, and his coat will lose the luster of youth. He may pass up a game of ball for a snooze in the sun. He is likely to develop a case of "selective hearing"—quite deaf most of the time but suddenly present when a bag of treats is opened. Other senses fail as well. The eyes often dim or become cloudy. Even his nose will no longer serve him as it did before. To keep him comfortable, safe and happy, he will need special care.

COMMON PROBLEMS

Arthritis and stiffening of the joints are common in old dogs. Your veterinarian can recommend medication to ease the discomfort. A soft, warm bed is a haven for him. Exercise is still important, but it should not go beyond moderate—perhaps a short walk at a slower pace. When he is pottering about on his own, watch that he does not bumble into a mishap or lose his way.

HELPING THE OLD CHAP OUT

The chapter on feeding describes options available for the older set. Look for good quality protein but less of it and fewer calories per serving. In spite of continued dental care throughout his life, his teeth may loosen and fall out, so soft food is appreciated. More frequent, smaller meals help the aging digestive system. He may drink more water and certainly will need to be taken out more often to spare his bladder undue stress. Extremes of temperature will be hard on him, and a sweater will keep him warm on his winter walks.

One thing that does not diminish with age is a Corgi's need for love and reassuring attention. Do not forget to boost his morale. Continue to include him in your daily life as much as possible.

Saying Good-Bye

The day will arrive when it is clear that your dog is no longer able to enjoy his life even in a scaled down version. Perhaps he will not eat, cannot get about at all or is in obvious pain. The indications are different for each animal. There is no need to prolong his suffering. He even may let you know he is ready. You have the option to ease his passage. You should discuss euthanasia with your veterinarian. He will advise you of the prognosis, but only you can make the decision to let your dog go, and it never is an easy one.

Be with your Corgi at the end. Hold him lovingly as you always have so he knows no fear. The doctor will give him a sedative and then inject a lethal dose of anesthetic. As life slips away know that together you have shared something very special—the bond between two best friends.

To grieve is natural. Each person does so in his own way. Do not let others chide you with "It was just a dog." You know better. Hang on to and treasure every memory. And some day, when you feel that the time is right for you, another furry little face may be licking yours.

Your Happy, Healthy Pet

Your Dog's Name _____

Name on Your Dog's Pedigree (if your dog has one) _____
_____

Where Your Dog Came From _____
_____

Your Dog's Birthday _____

Your Dog's Veterinarian

    Name _____
    Address _____
    Phone Number_____
    Emergency Number_____

Your Dog's Health

    Vaccines
    type _____ date given _____
    type _____ date given _____
    type _____ date given _____
    type _____ date given _____

    Heartworm
    date tested _____ type used_____ start date _____

Your Dog's License Number_____

Groomer's Name and Number _____

Dogsitter/Walker's Name and Number_____

Awards Your Dog Has Won

    Award _____ date earned _____
    Award _____ date earned _____

part three

Enjoying
your
Dog

8

Basic
Training

by Ian Dunbar, Ph.D., MRCVS

Training is the jewel in the crown—the most important aspect of doggy husbandry. There is no more important variable influencing dog behavior and temperament than the dog's education: A well-trained, well-behaved and good-natured puppydog is always a joy to live with, but an untrained and uncivilized dog can be a perpetual nightmare. Moreover, deny the dog an education and she will not have the opportunity to fulfill her own canine potential; neither will she have the ability to communicate effectively with her human companions.

Luckily, modern psychological training methods are easy, efficient, effective and, above all, considerably dog-friendly and user-friendly.

Doggy education is as simple as it is enjoyable. But before you can have a good time play-training with your new dog, you have to learn what to do and how to do it. There is no bigger variable influencing the success of dog training than the *owner's* experience and expertise. *Before you embark on the dog's education, you must first educate yourself.*

Basic Training for Owners

Ideally, basic owner training should begin well *before* you select your dog. Find out all you can about your chosen breed first, then master rudimentary training and handling skills. If you already have your puppy-dog, owner training is a dire emergency—the clock is ticking! Especially for puppies, the first few weeks at home are the most important and influential days in the dog's life. Indeed, the cause of most adolescent and adult problems may be traced back to the initial days the pup explores her new home. This is the time to establish the *status quo*—to teach the puppydog how you would like her to behave and so prevent otherwise quite predictable problems.

In addition to consulting breeders and breed books such as this one (which understandably have a positive breed bias), seek out as many pet owners with your breed as you can find. Good points are obvious. What you want to find out are the breed-specific *problems,* so you can nip them in the bud. In particular, you should talk to owners with *adolescent* dogs and make a list of all anticipated problems. Most important, *test drive* at least half a dozen adolescent and adult dogs of your breed yourself. An 8-week-old puppy is deceptively easy to handle, but she will acquire adult size, speed and strength in just four months, so you should learn now what to prepare for.

Puppy and pet dog training classes offer a convenient venue to locate pet owners and observe dogs in action. For a list of suitable trainers in your area, contact the Association of Pet Dog Trainers (see chapter 13). You may also begin your basic owner training by observing

other owners in class. Watch as many classes and test
drive as many dogs as possible. Select an upbeat, dog-
friendly, people-friendly, fun-and-games, puppydog pet
training class to learn the ropes. Also, watch training
videos and read training books. You must find out what
to do and how to do it *before* you have to do it.

Principles of Training

Most people think training comprises teaching the dog
to do things such as sit, speak and roll over, but even a
4-week-old pup knows how to do these things already.
Instead, the first step in training involves teaching
the dog human words for each dog behavior and activity and for each aspect of the dog's environment. That
way you, the owner, can more easily participate in the
dog's domestic education by directing her to perform
specific actions appropriately, that is, at the right time,
in the right place and so on. Training opens communication channels, enabling an educated dog to at least
understand her owner's requests.

In addition to teaching a dog *what* we want her to
do, it is also necessary to teach her *why* she should do
what we ask. Indeed, 95 percent of training revolves
around motivating the dog *to want to do* what we want.
Dogs often understand what their owners want; they
just don't see the point of doing it—especially when
the owner's repetitively boring and seemingly senseless
instructions are totally at odds with much more press-
ing and exciting doggy distractions. It is not so much
the dog that is being stubborn or dominant; rather, it
is the owner who has failed to acknowledge the dog's
needs and feelings and to approach training from the
dog's point of view.

THE MEANING OF INSTRUCTIONS

The secret to successful training is learning how to use
training lures to predict or prompt specific behaviors—
to coax the dog to do what you want *when* you want.
Any highly valued object (such as a treat or toy) may be
used as a lure, which the dog will follow with her eyes

and nose. Moving the lure in specific ways entices the dog to move her nose, head and entire body in specific ways. In fact, by learning the art of manipulating various lures, it is possible to teach the dog to assume virtually any body position and perform any action. Once you have control over the expression of the dog's behaviors and can elicit any body position or behavior at will, you can easily teach the dog to perform on request.

Teach your dog words for each activity she needs to know, like down.

Tell your dog what you want her to do, use a lure to entice her to respond correctly, then profusely praise and maybe reward her once she performs the desired action. For example, verbally request "Tina, sit!" while you move a squeaky toy upwards and backwards over the dog's muzzle (lure-movement and hand signal), smile knowingly as she looks up (to follow the lure) and sits down (as a result of canine anatomical engineering), then praise her to distraction ("Gooood Tina!"). Squeak the toy, offer a training treat and give your dog and yourself a pat on the back.

Being able to elicit desired responses over and over enables the owner to reward the dog over and over. Consequently, the dog begins to think training is fun. For example, the more the dog is rewarded for sitting, the more she enjoys sitting. Eventually the dog comes to realize that, whereas most sitting is appreciated, sitting immediately upon request usually prompts especially enthusiastic praise and a slew of high-level rewards. The dog begins to sit on cue much of the time, showing that she is starting to grasp the meaning of the owner's verbal request and hand signal.

WHY COMPLY?

Most dogs enjoy initial lure-reward training and are only too happy to comply with their owners' wishes. Unfortunately, repetitive drilling without appreciative feedback tends to diminish the dog's enthusiasm until she eventually fails to see the point of complying anymore. Moreover, as the dog approaches adolescence she becomes more easily distracted as she develops other interests. Lengthy sessions with repetitive exercises tend to bore and demotivate both parties. If it's not fun, the owner doesn't do it and neither does the dog.

Integrate training into your dog's life: The greater number of training sessions each day and the *shorter* they are, the more willingly compliant your dog will

To train your dog, you need gentle hands, a loving heart and a good attitude.

become. Make sure to have a short (just a few seconds) training interlude before every enjoyable canine activity. For example, ask your dog to sit to greet people, to sit before you throw her Frisbee and to sit for her supper. Really, sitting is no different from a canine "Please."

Also, include numerous short training interludes during every enjoyable canine pastime, for example, when playing with the dog or when she is running in the park. In this fashion, doggy distractions may be effectively converted into rewards for training. Just as all games have rules, fun becomes training . . . and training becomes fun.

Eventually, rewards actually become unnecessary to continue motivating your dog. If trained with consideration and kindness, performing the desired behaviors will become self-rewarding and, in a sense, your dog will motivate herself. Just as it is not necessary to reward a human companion during an enjoyable walk in the park, or following a game of tennis, it is hardly necessary to reward our best friend—the dog—for walking by our side or while playing fetch. Human company during enjoyable activities is reward enough for most dogs.

Even though your dog has become self-motivating, it's still good to praise and pet her a lot and offer rewards once in a while, especially for a good job well done. And if for no other reason, praising and rewarding others is good for the human heart.

PUNISHMENT

Without a doubt, lure-reward training is by far the best way to teach: Entice your dog to do what you want and then reward her for doing so. Unfortunately, a human shortcoming is to take the good for granted and to moan and groan at the bad. Specifically, the dog's many good behaviors are ignored while the owner focuses on punishing the dog for making mistakes. In extreme cases, instruction is *limited* to punishing mistakes made by a trainee dog, child, employee or husband, even though it has been proven punishment training is notoriously inefficient and ineffective and is decidedly unfriendly and combative. It teaches the dog that training is a drag, almost as quickly as it teaches the dog to dislike her trainer. Why treat our best friends like our worst enemies?

Punishment training is also much more laborious and time consuming. Whereas it takes only a finite amount of time to teach a dog what to chew, for example, it takes much, much longer to punish the dog for each and every mistake. Remember, *there is only one right way!* So why not teach that right way from the outset?!

To make matters worse, punishment training causes severe lapses in the dog's reliability. Since it is obviously impossible to punish the dog each and every time she misbehaves, the dog quickly learns to distinguish between those times when she must comply (so as to avoid impending punishment) and those times when she need not comply, because punishment is impossible. Such times include when the dog is off leash and 6 feet away, when the owner is otherwise engaged (talking to a friend, watching television, taking a shower, tending to the baby or chatting on the telephone) or when the dog is left at home alone.

Instances of misbehavior will be numerous when the owner is away, because even when the dog complied in the owner's looming presence, she did so unwillingly. The dog was forced to act against her will, rather than molding her will to want to please. Hence, when the owner is absent, not only does the dog know she need not comply, she simply does not want to. Again, the trainee is not a stubborn vindictive beast, but rather the trainer has failed to teach. Punishment training invariably creates unpredictable Jekyll and Hyde behavior.

Trainer's Tools

Many training books extol the virtues of a vast array of training paraphernalia and electronic and metallic gizmos, most of which are designed for canine restraint, correction and punishment, rather than for actual facilitation of doggy education. In reality, most effective training tools are not found in stores; they come from within ourselves. In addition to a willing dog, all you really need is a functional human brain, gentle hands, a loving heart and a good attitude.

In terms of equipment, all dogs do require a quality buckle collar to sport dog tags and to attach the leash (for safety and to comply with local leash laws). Hollow chew toys (like Kongs or sterilized longbones) and a dog bed or collapsible crate are musts for housetraining. Three additional tools are required:

1. specific lures (training treats and toys) to predict and prompt specific desired behaviors;
2. rewards (praise, affection, training treats and toys) to reinforce for the dog what a lot of fun it all is; and
3. knowledge—how to convert the dog's favorite activities and games (potential distractions to training) into "life-rewards," which may be employed to facilitate training.

The most powerful of these is *knowledge.* Education is the key! Watch training classes, participate in training classes, watch videos, read books, enjoy play-training with your dog and then your dog will say "Please," and your dog will say "Thank you!"

Housetraining

If dogs were left to their own devices, certainly they would chew, dig and bark for entertainment and then no doubt highlight a few areas of their living space with sprinkles of urine, in much the same way we decorate by hanging pictures. Consequently, when we ask a dog to live with us, we must teach her *where* she may dig, *where* she may perform her toilet duties, *what* she may chew and *when* she may bark. After all, when left at home alone for many hours, we cannot expect the dog to amuse herself by completing crosswords or watching the soaps on TV!

Also, it would be decidedly unfair to keep the house rules a secret from the dog, and then get angry and punish the poor critter for inevitably transgressing rules she did not even know existed. Remember: Without adequate education and guidance, the dog will be forced to establish her own rules—doggy rules—and most probably will be at odds with the owner's view of domestic living.

Since most problems develop during the first few days the dog is at home, prospective dog owners must be certain they are quite clear about the principles of housetraining *before* they get a dog. Early misbehaviors quickly become established as the *status quo—*

becoming firmly entrenched as hard-to-break bad habits, which set the precedent for years to come. Make sure to teach your dog good habits right from the start. Good habits are just as hard to break as bad ones!

Ideally, when a new dog comes home, try to arrange for someone to be present as much as possible during the first few days (for adult dogs) or weeks for puppies. With only a little forethought, it is surprisingly easy to find a puppy sitter, such as a retired person, who would be willing to eat from your refrigerator and watch your television while keeping an eye on the newcomer to encourage the dog to play with chew toys and to ensure she goes outside on a regular basis.

POTTY TRAINING

To teach the dog where to relieve herself:

1. never let her make a single mistake;
2. let her know where you want her to go; and
3. handsomely reward her for doing so: "GOOOOOOOD DOG!!!" liver treat, liver treat, liver treat!

Preventing Mistakes

A single mistake is a training disaster, since it heralds many more in future weeks. And each time the dog soils the house, this further reinforces the dog's unfortunate preference for an indoor, carpeted toilet. *Do not let an unhousetrained dog have full run of the house.*

When you are away from home, or cannot pay full attention, confine the dog to an area where elimination is appropriate, such as an outdoor run or, better still, a small, comfortable indoor kennel with access to an outdoor run. When confined in this manner, most dogs will naturally housetrain themselves.

If that's not possible, confine the dog to an area, such as a utility room, kitchen, basement or garage, where elimination may not be desired in the long run but as an interim measure it is certainly preferable to doing it all around the house. Use newspaper to cover the floor of the dog's day room. The newspaper may be used to soak up the urine and to wrap up and dispose of the feces. Once your dog develops a preferred spot for eliminating, it is only necessary to cover that part of the floor with newspaper. The smaller papered area may then be moved (only a little each day) towards the door to the outside. Thus the dog will develop the tendency to go to the door when she needs to relieve herself.

Never confine an unhousetrained dog to a crate for long periods. Doing so would force the dog to soil the crate and ruin its usefulness as an aid for housetraining (see the following discussion).

Teaching Where

In order to teach your dog where you would like her to do her business, you have to be there to direct the proceedings—an obvious, yet often neglected, fact of life. In order to be there

to teach the dog *where* to go, you need to know *when* she needs to go. Indeed, the success of housetraining depends on the owner's ability to predict these times. Certainly, a regular feeding schedule will facilitate prediction somewhat, but there is nothing like "loading the deck" and influencing the timing of the outcome yourself!

Whenever you are at home, make sure the dog is under constant supervision and/or confined to a small

The first few weeks at home are the most important and influential in your dog's life.

area. If already well trained, simply instruct the dog to lie down in her bed or basket. Alternatively, confine the dog to a crate (doggy den) or tie-down (a short, 18-inch lead that can be clipped to an eye hook in the baseboard near her bed). Short-term close confinement strongly inhibits urination and defecation, since the dog does not want to soil her sleeping area. Thus, when you release the puppydog each hour, she will definitely need to urinate immediately and defecate every third or fourth hour. Keep the dog confined to her doggy den and take her to her intended toilet area each hour, every hour and on the hour.

When taking your dog outside, instruct her to sit quietly before opening the door—she will soon learn to sit by the door when she needs to go out!

Teaching Why

Being able to predict when the dog needs to go enables the owner to be on the spot to praise and reward the dog. Each hour, hurry the dog to the intended toilet area in the yard, issue the appropriate instruction ("Go pee!" or "Go poop!"), then give the dog three to four minutes to produce. Praise and offer a couple of training treats when successful. The treats are important because many people fail to praise their dogs with feeling . . . and housetraining is hardly the time for understatement. So either loosen up and enthusiastically praise that dog: "Wuzzzer-wuzzer-wuzzer, hoooser good wuffer den? Hoooo went pee for Daddy?" Or say "Good dog!" as best you can and offer the treats for effect.

Following elimination is an ideal time for a spot of play-training in the yard or house. Also, an empty dog may be allowed greater freedom around the house for the next half hour or so, just as long as you keep an eye out to make sure she does not get into other kinds of mischief. If you are preoccupied and cannot pay full attention, confine the dog to her doggy den once more to enjoy a peaceful snooze or to play with her many chew toys.

If your dog does not eliminate within the allotted time outside—no biggie! Back to her doggy den, and then try again after another hour.

As I own large dogs, I always feel more relaxed walking an empty dog, knowing that I will not need to finish our stroll weighted down with bags of feces!

Beware of falling into the trap of walking the dog to get her to eliminate. The good ol' dog walk is such an enormous highlight in the dog's life that it represents the single biggest potential reward in domestic dogdom. However, when in a hurry, or during inclement weather, many owners abruptly terminate the walk the moment the dog has done her business. This, in effect, severely punishes the dog for doing the right thing, in the right place at the right time. Consequently, many dogs become strongly inhibited from eliminating outdoors because they know it will signal an abrupt end to an otherwise thoroughly enjoyable walk.

Instead, instruct the dog to relieve herself in the yard prior to going for a walk. If you follow the above instructions, most dogs soon learn to eliminate on cue. As soon as the dog eliminates, praise (and offer a treat or two)—"Good dog! Let's go walkies!" Use the walk as a reward for eliminating in the yard. If the dog does not go, put her back in her doggy den and think about a walk later on. You will find with a "No feces—no walk" policy, your dog will become one of the fastest defecators in the business.

If you do not have a backyard, instruct the dog to eliminate right outside your front door prior to the walk. Not only will this facilitate clean up and disposal of the feces in your own trash can but, also, the walk may again be used as a colossal reward.

CHEWING AND BARKING

Short-term close confinement also teaches the dog that occasional quiet moments are a reality of domestic living. Your puppydog is extremely impressionable during her first few weeks at home. Regular confinement at this time soon exerts a calming influence over the dog's personality. Remember, once the dog is housetrained and calmer, there will be a whole lifetime ahead for the dog to enjoy full run of the house and garden. On the other hand, by letting the newcomer have unrestricted access to the entire household and allowing her to run willy-nilly, she will most certainly develop a bunch of behavior problems in short order, no doubt necessitating confinement later in life. It would not be fair to remedially restrain and confine a dog you have trained, through neglect, to run free.

When confining the dog, make sure she always has an impressive array of suitable chew toys. Kongs and sterilized longbones (both readily available from pet stores) make the best chew toys, since they are hollow and may be stuffed with treats to heighten the dog's interest. For example, by stuffing the little hole at the top of a Kong with a small piece of freeze-dried liver, the dog will not want to leave it alone.

Remember, treats do not have to be junk food and they certainly should not represent extra calories. Rather, treats should be part of each dog's regular daily diet: Some food may be served in the dog's bowl for breakfast and dinner, some food may be used as training treats, and some food may be used for stuffing chew toys. I regularly stuff my dogs' many Kongs with different shaped biscuits and kibble.

Make sure your puppy has suitable chew toys.

The kibble seems to fall out fairly easily, as do the oval-shaped biscuits, thus rewarding the dog instantaneously for checking out the chew toys. The bone-shaped biscuits fall out after a while, rewarding the dog for worrying at the chew toy. But the triangular biscuits never come out. They remain inside the Kong as lures, maintaining the dog's fascination with her chew toy. To further focus the dog's interest, I always make sure to flavor the triangular biscuits by rubbing them with a little cheese or freeze-dried liver.

If stuffed chew toys are reserved especially for times the dog is confined, the puppydog will soon learn to enjoy quiet moments in her doggy den and she will quickly develop a chew-toy habit— a good habit! This is a simple *autoshaping* process; all the owner has to do is set up the situation and the dog all but trains herself— easy and effective. Even when the dog is given run of the house, her first inclination will be to indulge her rewarding chew-toy habit rather than destroy less-attractive household articles, such as curtains, carpets, chairs and compact disks. Similarly, a chew-toy chewer will be less inclined to scratch and chew herself excessively. Also, if the dog busies herself as a recreational chewer, she will be less inclined to develop into a recreational barker or digger when left at home alone.

Stuff a number of chew toys whenever the dog is left confined and remove the extra-special-tasting treats when you return. Your dog will now amuse herself with her chew toys before falling asleep and then resume playing with her chew toys when she expects you to return. Since most owner-absent misbehavior happens right after you leave and right before your expected return, your puppydog will now be conveniently preoccupied with her chew toys at these times.

Come and Sit

Most puppies will happily approach virtually anyone, whether called or not; that is, until they collide with adolescence and

develop other more important doggy interests, such as sniffing a multiplicity of exquisite odors on the grass. Your mission, Mr./Ms. Owner, is to teach and reward the pup for coming reliably, willingly and happily when called—and you have just three months to get it done. Unless adequately reinforced, your puppy's tendency to approach people will self-destruct by adolescence.

Call your dog ("Tina, come!"), open your arms (and maybe squat down) as a welcoming signal, waggle a treat or toy as a lure and reward the puppydog when she comes running. Do not wait to praise the dog until she reaches you—she may come 95 percent of the way and then run off after some distraction. Instead, praise the dog's *first* step towards you and continue praising enthusiastically for *every* step she takes in your direction.

When the rapidly approaching puppy dog is three lengths away from impact, instruct her to sit ("Tina, sit!") and hold the lure in front of you in an outstretched hand to prevent her from hitting you midchest and knocking you flat on your back! As Tina decelerates to nose the lure, move the treat upwards and backwards just over her muzzle with an upwards motion of your extended arm (palm-upwards). As the dog looks up to follow the lure, she will sit down (if she jumps up, you are holding the lure too high). Praise the dog for sitting. Move backwards and call her again. Repeat this many times over, always praising when Tina comes and sits; on occasion, reward her.

For the first couple of trials, use a training treat both as a lure to entice the dog to come and sit and as a reward for doing so. Thereafter, try to use different items as lures and rewards. For example, lure the dog with a Kong or Frisbee but reward her with a food treat. Or lure the dog with a food treat but pat her and throw a tennis ball as a reward. After just a few repetitions, dispense with the lures and rewards; the dog will begin to respond willingly to your verbal requests and hand signals just for the prospect of praise from your heart and affection from your hands.

Instruct every family member, friend and visitor how to get the dog to come and sit. Invite people over for a series of pooch parties; do not keep the pup a secret— let other people enjoy this puppy, and let the pup enjoy other people. Puppydog parties are not only fun, they easily attract a lot of people to help *you* train *your* dog. Unless you teach your dog how to meet people, that is, to sit for greetings, no doubt the dog will resort to jumping up. Then you and the visitors will get annoyed, and the dog will be punished. This is not fair. *Send out those invitations for puppy parties and teach your dog to be mannerly and socially acceptable.*

Even though your dog quickly masters obedient recalls in the house, her reliability may falter when playing in the backyard or local park. Ironically, it is *the owner* who has unintentionally trained the dog *not* to respond in these instances. By allowing the dog to play and run around and otherwise have a good time, but then to call the dog to put her on leash to take her home, the dog quickly learns playing is fun but training is a drag. Thus, playing in the park becomes a severe distraction, which works against training. Bad news!

Instead, whether playing with the dog off leash or on leash, request her to come at frequent intervals—say, every minute or so. On most occasions, praise and pet the dog for a few seconds while she is sitting, then tell her to go play again. For especially fast recalls, offer a couple of training treats and take the time to praise and pet the dog enthusiastically before releasing her. The dog will learn that coming when called is not necessarily the end of the play session, and neither is it the end of the world; rather, it signals an enjoyable, quality time-out with the owner before resuming play once more. In fact, playing in the park now becomes a very effective life-reward, which works to facilitate training by reinforcing each obedient and timely recall. Good news!

Sit, Down, Stand and Rollover

Teaching the dog a variety of body positions is easy for owner and dog, impressive for spectators and extremely useful for all. Using lure-reward techniques, it is possible to train several positions at once to verbal commands or hand signals (which impress the socks off onlookers).

Sit and ***down***—the two control commands—prevent or resolve nearly a hundred behavior problems. For example, if the dog happily and obediently sits or lies down when requested, she cannot jump on visitors, dash out the front door, run around and chase her tail, pester other dogs, harass cats or annoy family, friends or strangers. Additionally, "Sit" or "Down" are the best emergency commands for off-leash control.

It is easier to teach and maintain a reliable sit than maintain a reliable recall. *Sit* is the purest and simplest of commands—either the dog is sitting or she is not. If there is any change of circumstances or potential danger in the park, for example, simply instruct the dog to sit. If she sits, you have a number of options: Allow the dog to resume playing when she is safe, walk up and put the dog on leash or call the dog. The dog will be much more likely to come when called if she has already acknowledged her compliance by sitting. If the dog does not sit in the park—train her to!

Stand and ***rollover-stay*** are the two positions for examining the dog. Your veterinarian will love you to distraction if you take a little time to teach the dog to stand still and roll over and play possum. Also, your vet bills will be smaller because it will take the veterinarian less time to examine your dog. The rollover-stay is an especially useful command and is really just a variation of the down-stay: Whereas the dog lies prone in the traditional down, she lies supine in the rollover-stay.

As with teaching come and sit, the training techniques to teach the dog to assume all other body positions on cue are user-friendly and dog-friendly. Simply give the appropriate request, lure the dog into the desired body position using a training treat or toy and then *praise* (and maybe reward) the dog as soon as she complies. Try not to touch the dog to get her to respond. If you teach the dog by guiding her into position, the dog will quickly learn that rump-pressure means sit, for example, but as yet you still have no control over your dog if she is just 6 feet away. It will still be necessary to teach the dog to sit on request. So do not make training a time-consuming two-step process; instead, teach the dog to sit to a verbal request or hand signal from the outset. Once the dog sits willingly when requested, by all means use your hands to pet the dog when she does so.

To teach *down* when the dog is already sitting, say "Tina, down!," hold the lure in one hand (palm down) and lower that hand to the floor between the dog's forepaws. As the dog lowers her head to follow the lure, slowly move the lure away from the dog just a fraction (in front of her paws). The dog will lie down as she stretches her nose forward to follow the lure. Praise the dog when she does so. If the dog stands up, you pulled the lure away too far and too quickly.

When teaching the dog to lie down from the standing position, say "Down" and lower the lure to the floor as before. Once the dog has lowered her forequarters and assumed a play bow, gently and slowly move the lure *towards* the dog between her forelegs. Praise the dog as soon as her rear end plops down.

After just a couple of trials it will be possible to alternate sits and downs and have the dog energetically perform doggy push-ups. Praise the dog a lot, and after half a dozen or so push-ups reward the dog with a training treat or toy. You will notice the more energetically you move your arm—upwards (palm up) to get the dog to sit, and downwards (palm down) to get the dog to lie down—the more energetically the dog responds to your requests. Now try training the dog in silence and you will notice she has also learned to respond to hand signals. Yeah! Not too shabby for the first session.

To teach *stand* from the sitting position, say "Tina, stand," slowly move the lure half a dog-length away from the dog's nose, keeping it at nose level, and praise the dog as she stands to follow the lure. As soon

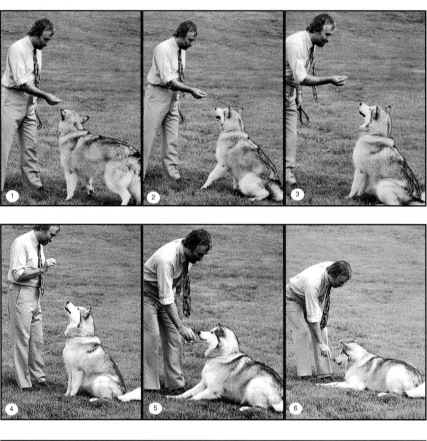

Using a food lure to teach sit, down and stand. 1) "Phoenix, sit." 2) Hand palm upwards, move lure up and back over dog's muzzle. 3) "Good sit, Phoenix!" 4) "Phoenix, down." 5) Hand palm downwards, move lure down to lie between dog's forepaws. 6) "Phoenix, off. Good down, Phoenix!" 7) "Phoenix, sit!" 8) Palm upwards, move lure up and back, keeping it close to dog's muzzle. 9) "Good sit, Phoenix!"

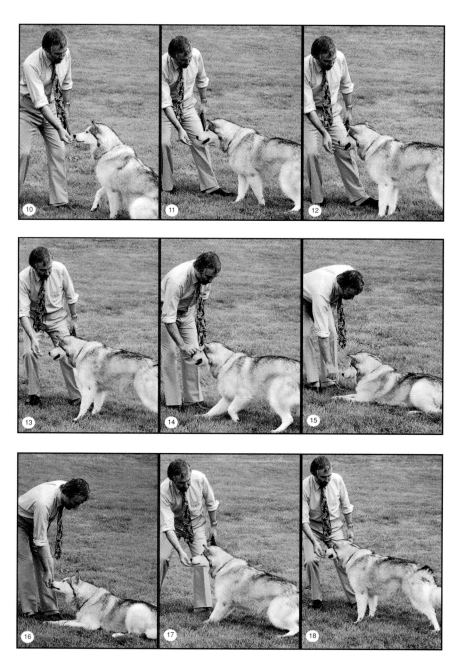

10) *"Phoenix, stand!"* 11) *Move lure away from dog at nose height, then lower it a tad.* 12) *"Phoenix, off! Good stand, Phoenix!"* 13) *"Phoenix, down!"* 14) *Hand palm downwards, move lure down to lie between dog's forepaws.* 15) *"Phoenix, off! Good down-stay, Phoenix!"* 16) *"Phoenix, stand!"* 17) *Move lure away from dog's muzzle up to nose height.* 18) *"Phoenix, off! Good stand-stay, Phoenix. Now we'll make the vet and groomer happy!"*

as the dog stands, lower the lure to just beneath the dog's chin to entice her to look down; otherwise she will stand and then sit immediately. To prompt the dog to stand from the down position, move the lure half a dog-length upwards and away from the dog, holding the lure at standing nose height from the floor.

Teaching *rollover* is best started from the down position, with the dog lying on one side, or at least with both hind legs stretched out on the same side. Say "Tina, bang!" and move the lure backwards and alongside the dog's muzzle to her elbow (on the side of her outstretched hind legs). Once the dog looks to the side and backwards, very slowly move the lure upwards to the dog's shoulder and backbone. Tickling the dog in the goolies (groin area) often invokes a reflex-raising of the hind leg as an appeasement gesture, which facilitates the tendency to roll over. If you move the lure too quickly and the dog jumps into the standing position, have patience and start again. As soon as the dog rolls onto her back, keep the lure stationary and mesmerize the dog with a relaxing tummy rub.

To teach *rollover-stay* when the dog is standing or moving, say "Tina, bang!" and give the appropriate hand signal (with index finger pointed and thumb cocked in true Sam Spade fashion), then in one fluid movement lure her to first lie down and then rollover-stay as above.

Teaching the dog to *stay* in each of the above four positions becomes a piece of cake after first teaching the dog not to worry at the toy or treat training lure. This is best accomplished by hand feeding dinner kibble. Hold a piece of kibble firmly in your hand and softly instruct "Off!" Ignore any licking and slobbering *for however long the dog worries at the treat,* but say "Take it!" and offer the kibble *the instant* the dog breaks contact with her muzzle. Repeat this a few times, and then up the ante and insist the dog remove her muzzle for one whole second before offering the kibble. Then progressively refine your criteria and have the dog not touch your hand (or treat) for longer and longer periods on each trial, such as for two seconds, four seconds, then six, ten, fifteen, twenty, thirty seconds and so on.

The dog soon learns: (1) worrying at the treat never gets results, whereas (2) noncontact is often rewarded after a variable time lapse.

Teaching *"Off!"* has many useful applications in its own right. Additionally, instructing the dog not to touch a training lure often produces spontaneous and magical stays. Request the dog to stand-stay, for example, and not to touch the lure. At first set your sights on a short two-second stay before rewarding the dog. (Remember, every long journey begins with a single step.) However, on subsequent trials, gradually and progressively increase the length of stay required to receive a reward. In no time at all your dog will stand calmly for a minute or so.

Relevancy Training

Once you have taught the dog what you expect her to do when requested to come, sit, lie down, stand, rollover and stay, the time is right to teach the dog *why* she should comply with your wishes. The secret is to have many (*many*) extremely short training interludes (two to five seconds each) at numerous (*numerous*) times during the course of the dog's day. Especially work with the dog immediately *before* the dog's good times and *during* the dog's good times. For example, ask your dog to sit and/or lie down each time before opening doors, serving meals, offering treats and tummy rubs; ask the dog to perform a few controlled doggy push-ups before letting her off leash or throwing a tennis ball; and perhaps request the dog to sit-down-sit-stand-down-stand-rollover before inviting her to cuddle on the couch.

Similarly, request the dog to sit many times during play or on walks, and in no time at all the dog will be only too pleased to follow your instructions because she has learned that a compliant response heralds all sorts of goodies. Basically all you are trying to teach the dog is how to say please: "Please throw the tennis ball. Please may I snuggle on the couch."

Remember, it is important to keep training interludes short and to have many short sessions each and every day. The shortest (and most useful) session comprises asking the dog to sit and then go play during a play session. When trained this way, your dog will soon associate training with good times. In fact, the dog may be unable to distinguish between training and good times and, indeed, there should be no distinction. The warped concept that training involves forcing the dog to comply and/or dominating her will is totally at odds with the picture of a truly well-trained dog. In reality, enjoying a game of training with a dog is no different from enjoying a game of backgammon or tennis with a friend; and walking with a dog should be no different from strolling with a spouse, or with buddies on the golf course.

Walk by Your Side

Many people attempt to teach a dog to heel by putting her on a leash and physically correcting the dog when she makes mistakes. There are a number of things seriously wrong with this approach, the first being that most people do not want precision heeling; rather, they simply want the dog to follow or walk by their side. Second, when physically restrained during "training," even though the dog may grudgingly mope by your side when "handcuffed" on leash, let's see what happens when she is off leash. History! The dog is in the next county because she never enjoyed walking with you on leash and you have no control over her off leash. So let's just teach the dog off leash from the outset to *want* to walk with us. Third, if the dog has not been trained to heel, it is a trifle hasty to think about punishing the poor dog for making mistakes and breaking heeling rules she didn't even know existed. This is simply not fair! Surely, if the dog had been adequately taught how to heel, she would seldom make mistakes and hence there would be no need to correct the dog. Remember, each mistake and each correction (punishment) advertise the trainer's inadequacy, not the dog's. The dog is not stubborn, she is not stupid and she is not bad. Even if she were, she would still require training, so let's train her properly.

Let's teach the dog to *enjoy* following us and to *want* to walk by our side off leash. Then it will be easier to teach high-precision off-leash heeling patterns if desired. Before going on outdoor walks, it is necessary to teach the dog not to pull. Then it becomes easy to teach on-leash walking and heeling because the dog already wants to walk with you, she is familiar with the desired walking and heeling positions and she knows not to pull.

FOLLOWING

Start by training your dog to follow you. Many puppies will follow if you simply walk away from them and maybe click your fingers or chuckle. Adult dogs may require additional enticement to stimulate them to follow, such as a training lure or, at the very least, a lively trainer. To teach the dog to follow: (1) keep walking and (2) walk away from the dog. If the dog attempts to lead or lag, change pace; slow down if the dog forges too far ahead, but speed up if she lags too far behind. Say "Steady!" or "Easy!" each time before you slow down and "Quickly!" or "Hustle!" each time before you speed up, and the dog will learn to change pace on cue. If the dog lags or leads too far, or if she wanders right or left, simply walk quickly in the opposite direction and maybe even run away from the dog and hide.

Practicing is a lot of fun; you can set up a course in your home, yard or park to do this. Indoors, entice the dog to follow upstairs, into a bedroom, into the bathroom, downstairs, around the living room couch, zigzagging between dining room chairs and into the kitchen for dinner. Outdoors, get the dog to follow around park benches, trees, shrubs and along walkways and lines in the grass. (For safety outdoors, it is advisable to attach a long line on the dog, but never exert corrective tension on the line.)

121

Remember, following has a lot to do with attitude—
your attitude! Most probably your dog will *not* want to
follow Mr. Grumpy Troll with the personality of wilted
lettuce. Lighten up—walk with a jaunty step, whistle a
happy tune, sing, skip and tell jokes to your dog and
she will be right there by your side.

BY YOUR SIDE

It is smart to train the dog to walk close on one side or
the other—either side will do, your choice. When walking, jogging or cycling, it is generally bad news to have
the dog suddenly cut in front of you. In fact, I train my
dogs to walk "By my side" and "Other side"—both very
useful instructions. It is possible to position the dog
fairly accurately by looking to the appropriate side and
clicking your fingers or slapping your thigh on that
side. A precise positioning may be attained by holding
a training lure, such as a chew toy, tennis ball or food
treat. Stop and stand still several times throughout the
walk, just as you would when window shopping or
meeting a friend. Use the lure to make sure the dog
slows down and stays close whenever you stop.

When teaching the dog to heel, we generally want
her to sit in heel position when we stop. Teach heel

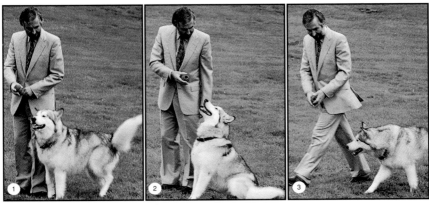

Using a toy to teach sit-heel-sit sequences: 1) "Phoenix, sit!" Standing still, move lure up and back over dog's muzzle . . . 2) to position dog sitting in heel position on your left side. 3) Say "Phoenix, heel!" and walk ahead, wagging lure in left hand. Change lure to right hand in preparation for sit signal. Say "Sit" and then . . .

122

position at the standstill and the dog will learn that the default heel position is sitting by your side (left or right—your choice, unless you wish to compete in obedience trials, in which case the dog must heel on the left).

Several times a day, stand up and call your dog to come and sit in heel position—"Tina, heel!" For example, instruct the dog to come to heel each time there are commercials on TV, or each time you turn a page of a novel, and the dog will get it in a single evening.

Practice straight-line heeling and turns separately. With the dog sitting at heel, teach her to turn in place. After each quarter-turn, half-turn or full turn in place, lure the dog to sit at heel. Now it's time for short straight-line heeling sequences, no more than a few steps at a time. Always think of heeling in terms of sit-heel-sit sequences—start and end with the dog in position and do your best to keep her there when moving. Progressively increase the number of steps in each sequence. When the dog remains close for 20 yards of straight-line heeling, it is time to add a few turns and then sign up for a happy-heeling obedience class to get some advice from the experts.

4) use hand signal to lure dog to sit as you stop. Eventually, dog will sit automatically at heel whenever you stop. 5) "Good dog!"

No Pulling on Leash

You can start teaching your dog not to pull on leash anywhere—in front of the television or outdoors—but regardless of location, you must not take a single step with tension in the leash. For a reason known only to dogs, even just a couple of paces of pulling on leash is intrinsically motivating and diabolically rewarding. Instead, attach the leash to the dog's collar, grasp the other end firmly with both hands held close to your chest, and stand still—do not budge an inch. Have somebody watch you with a stopwatch to time your progress, or else you will never believe this will work and so you will not even try the exercise, and your shoulder and the dog's neck will be traumatized for years to come.

Stand still and wait for the dog to stop pulling, and to sit and/or lie down. All dogs stop pulling and sit eventually. Most take only a couple of minutes; the all-time record is 22½ minutes. Time how long it takes. Gently praise the dog when she stops pulling, and as soon as she sits, enthusiastically praise the dog and take just one step forward, then immediately stand still. This single step usually demonstrates the ballistic reinforcing nature of pulling on leash; most dogs explode to the end of the leash, so be prepared for the strain. Stand firm and wait for the dog to sit again. Repeat this half a dozen times and you will probably notice a progressive reduction in the force of the dog's one-step explosions and a radical reduction in the time it takes for the dog to sit each time.

As the dog learns "Sit we go" and "Pull we stop," she will begin to walk forward calmly with each single step and automatically sit when you stop. Now try two steps before you stop. Wooooooo! Scary! When the dog has mastered two steps at a time, try for three. After each success, progressively increase the number of steps in the sequence: try four steps and then six, eight, ten and twenty steps before stopping. Congratulations! You are now walking the dog on leash.

Whenever walking with the dog (off leash or on leash), make sure you stop periodically to practice a few position commands and stays before instructing the dog to "Walk on!" (Remember, you want the dog to be compliant everywhere, not just in the kitchen when her dinner is at hand.) For example, stopping every 25 yards to briefly train the dog amounts to over 200 training interludes within a single 3-mile stroll. And each training session is in a different location. You will not believe the improvement within just the first mile of the first walk.

To put it another way, integrating training into a walk offers 200 separate opportunities to use the continuance of the walk as a reward to reinforce the dog's education. Moreover, some training interludes may comprise continuing education for the dog's walking skills: Alternate short periods of the dog walking calmly by your side with periods when the dog is allowed to sniff and investigate the environment. Now sniffing odors on the grass and meeting other dogs become rewards which reinforce the dog's calm and mannerly demeanor. Good Lord! Whatever next? Many enjoyable walks together of course. Happy trails!

THE IMPORTANCE OF TRICKS

Nothing will improve a dog's quality of life better than having a few tricks under her belt. Teaching any trick expands the dog's vocabulary, which facilitates communication and improves the owner's control. Also, specific tricks help prevent and resolve specific behavior problems. For example, by teaching the dog to fetch her toys, the dog learns carrying a toy makes the owner happy and, therefore, will be more likely to chew her toy than other inappropriate items.

More important, teaching tricks prompts owners to lighten up and train with a sunny disposition. Really, tricks should be no different from any other behaviors we put on cue. But they are. When teaching tricks, owners have a much sweeter attitude, which in turn motivates the dog and improves her willingness to comply. The dog feels tricks are a blast, but formal commands are a drag. In fact, tricks are so enjoyable, they may be used as rewards in training by asking the dog to come, sit and down-stay and then rollover for a tummy rub. Go on, try it: Crack a smile and even giggle when the dog promptly and willingly lies down and stays.

Most important, performing tricks prompts onlookers to smile and giggle. Many people are scared of dogs, especially large ones. And nothing can be more off-putting for a dog than to be constantly confronted by strangers who don't like her because of her size or the way she looks. Uneasy people put the dog on edge, causing her to back off and bark, only frightening people all the more. And so a vicious circle develops, with the people's fear fueling the dog's fear *and vice versa*. Instead, tie a pink ribbon to your dog's collar and practice all sorts of tricks on walks and in the park, and you will be pleasantly amazed how it changes people's attitudes toward your friendly dog. The dog's repertoire of tricks is limited only by the trainer's imagination. Below I have described three of my favorites:

SPEAK AND SHUSH

The training sequence involved in teaching a dog to bark on request is no different from that used when training any behavior on cue: request—lure—response—reward. As always, the secret of success lies in finding an effective lure. If the dog always barks at the doorbell, for example, say "Rover, speak!", have an accomplice ring the doorbell, then reward the dog for barking. After a few woofs, ask Rover to "Shush!", waggle a food treat under her nose (to entice her to sniff and thus to shush), praise her when quiet and eventually offer the treat as a reward. Alternate "Speak" and "Shush," progressively increasing the length of shush-time between each barking bout.

PLAY BOW

With the dog standing, say "Bow!" and lower the food lure (palm upwards) to rest between the dog's forepaws. Praise as the dog lowers

her forequarters and sternum to the ground (as when teaching the down), but then lure the dog to stand and offer the treat. On successive trials, gradually increase the length of time the dog is required to remain in the play bow posture in order to gain a food reward. If the dog's rear end collapses into a down, say nothing and offer no reward; simply start over.

BE A BEAR

With the dog sitting backed into a corner to prevent her from toppling over backwards, say "Be a bear!" With bent paw and palm down, raise a lure upwards and backwards along the top of the dog's muzzle. Praise the dog when she sits up on her haunches and offer the treat as a reward. To prevent the dog from standing on her hind legs, keep the lure closer to the dog's muzzle. On each trial, progressively increase the length of time the dog is required to sit up to receive a food reward. Since lure-reward training is so easy, teach the dog to stand and walk on her hind legs as well!

Teaching "Be a Bear"

chapter 9

Getting
Active
with your Dog
by Bardi McLennan

Once you and your dog have graduated from basic obedience training and are beginning to work together as a team, you can take part in the growing world of dog activities. There are so many fun things to do with your dog! Just remember, people and dogs don't always learn at the same pace, so don't be upset if you (or your dog) need more than two basic training courses before your team becomes operational. Even smart dogs don't go straight to college from kindergarten!

Just as there are events geared to certain types of dogs, so there are ones that are more appealing to certain types of people. In some

128

activities, you give the commands and your dog does the work (upland game hunting is one example), while in others, such as agility, you'll both get a workout. You may want to aim for prestigious titles to add to your dog's name, or you may want nothing more than the sheer enjoyment of being around other people and their dogs. Passive or active, participation has its own rewards.

Consider your dog's physical capabilities when looking into any of the canine activities. It's easy to see that a Basset Hound is not built for the racetrack, nor would a Chihuahua be the breed of choice for pulling a sled. A loyal dog will attempt almost anything you ask him to do, so it is up to you to know your dog's limitations. A dog must be physically sound in order to compete at any level in athletic activities, and being mentally sound is a definite plus. Advanced age, however, may not be a deterrent. Many dogs still hunt and herd at ten or twelve years of age. It's entirely possible for dogs to be "fit at 50." Take your dog for a checkup, explain to your vet the type of activity you have in mind and be guided by his or her findings.

All dogs seem to love playing flyball.

You needn't be restricted to breed-specific sports if it's only fun you're after. Certain AKC activities are limited to designated breeds; however, as each new trial, test or sport has grown in popularity, so has the variety of breeds encouraged to participate at a fun level.

But don't shortchange your fun, or that of your dog, by thinking only of the basic function of her breed. Once a dog has learned how to learn, she can be taught to do just about anything as long as the size of the dog is right for the job and you both think it is fun and rewarding. In other words, you are a team.

To get involved in any of the activities detailed in this chapter, look for the names and addresses of the organizations that sponsor them in Chapter 13. You can also ask your breeder or a local dog trainer for contacts.

You can compete in obedience trials with a well trained dog.

Official American Kennel Club Activities

The following tests and trials are some of the events sanctioned by the AKC and sponsored by various dog clubs. Your dog's expertise will be rewarded with impressive titles. You can participate just for fun, or be competitive and go for those awards.

OBEDIENCE

Training classes begin with pups as young as three months of age in kindergarten puppy training, then advance to pre-novice (all exercises on lead) and go on to novice, which is where you'll start off-lead work. In obedience classes dogs learn to sit, stay, heel and come through a variety of exercises. Once you've got the basics down, you can enter obedience trials and work toward earning your dog's first degree, a C.D. (Companion Dog).

The next level is called "Open," in which jumps and retrieves perk up the dog's interest. Passing grades in competition at this level earn a C.D.X. (Companion Dog Excellent). Beyond that lies the goal of the most ambitious—Utility (U.D. and even U.D.X. or OTCh, an Obedience Champion).

AGILITY

All dogs can participate in the latest canine sport to have gained worldwide popularity for its fun and excitement, agility. It began in England as a canine version of horse show-jumping, but because dogs are more agile and able to perform on verbal commands, extra feats were added such as climbing, balancing and racing through tunnels or in and out of weave poles. Many of the obstacles (regulation or homemade) can be set up in your own backyard. If the agility bug bites, you could end up in international competition!

For starters, your dog should be obedience trained, even though, in the beginning, the lessons may all be taught on lead. Once the dog understands the commands (and you do, too), it's as easy as guiding the dog over a prescribed course, one obstacle at a time. In competition, the race is against the clock, so wear your running shoes! The dog starts with 200 points and the judge deducts for infractions and misadventures along the way.

All dogs seem to love agility and respond to it as if they were being turned loose in a playground paradise. Your dog's enthusiasm will be contagious; agility turns into great fun for dog and owner.

FIELD TRIALS AND HUNTING TESTS

There are field trials and hunting tests for the sporting breeds—retrievers, spaniels and pointing breeds, and for some hounds—Bassets, Beagles and Dachshunds. Field trials are competitive events that test a dog's ability to perform the functions for which she was bred. Hunting tests, which are open to retrievers,

---

TITLES AWARDED BY THE AKC

Conformation: Ch. (Champion)

Obedience: CD (Companion Dog); CDX (Companion Dog Excellent); UD (Utility Dog); UDX (Utility Dog Excellent); OTCh. (Obedience Trial Champion)

Field: JH (Junior Hunter); SH (Senior Hunter); MH (Master Hunter); AFCh. (Amateur Field Champion); FCh. (Field Champion)

Lure Coursing: JC (Junior Courser); SC (Senior Courser)

Herding: HT (Herding Tested); PT (Pre-Trial Tested); HS (Herding Started); HI (Herding Intermediate); HX (Herding Excellent); HCh. (Herding Champion)

Tracking: TD (Tracking Dog); TDX (Tracking Dog Excellent)

Agility: NAD (Novice Agility); OAD (Open Agility); ADX (Agility Excellent); MAX (Master Agility)

Earthdog Tests: JE (Junior Earthdog); SE (Senior Earthdog); ME (Master Earthdog)

Canine Good Citizen: CGC

Combination: DC (Dual Champion—Ch. and Fch.); TC (Triple Champion—Ch., Fch., and OTCh.)

spaniels and pointing breeds only, are noncompetitive and are a means of judging the dog's ability as well as that of the handler.

Hunting is a very large and complex part of canine sports, and if you own one of the breeds that hunts, the events are a great treat for your dog and you. He gets to do what he was bred for, and you get to work with him and watch him do it. You'll be proud of and amazed at what your dog can do.

Fortunately, the AKC publishes a series of booklets on these events, which outline the rules and regulations and include a glossary of the sometimes complicated terms. The AKC also publishes newsletters for field trialers and hunting test enthusiasts. The United Kennel Club (UKC) also has informative materials for the hunter and his dog.

Retrievers and other sporting breeds get to do what they're bred to in hunting tests.

HERDING TESTS AND TRIALS

Herding, like hunting, dates back to the first known uses man made of dogs. The interest in herding today is widespread, and if you own a herding breed, you can join in the activity. Herding dogs are tested for their natural skills to keep a flock of ducks, sheep or cattle together. If your dog shows potential, you can start at the testing level, where your dog can earn a title for showing an inherent herding ability. With training you can advance to the trial level, where your dog should be capable of controlling even difficult livestock in diverse situations.

LURE COURSING

The AKC Tests and Trials for Lure Coursing are open to traditional sighthounds—Greyhounds, Whippets,

Borzoi, Salukis, Afghan Hounds, Ibizan Hounds and Scottish Deerhounds—as well as to Basenjis and Rhodesian Ridgebacks. Hounds are judged on overall ability, follow, speed, agility and endurance. This is possibly the most exciting of the trials for spectators, because the speed and agility of the dogs is awesome to watch as they chase the lure (or "course") in heats of two or three dogs at a time.

Tracking

Tracking is another activity in which almost any dog can compete because every dog that sniffs the ground when taken outdoors is, in fact, tracking. The hard part comes when the rules as to what, when and where the dog tracks are determined by a person, not the dog! Tracking tests cover a large area of fields, woods and roads. The tracks are laid hours before the dogs go to work on them, and include "tricks" like cross-tracks and sharp turns. If you're interested in search-and-rescue work, this is the place to start.

This tracking dog is hot on the trail.

Earthdog Tests for Small Terriers and Dachshunds

These tests are open to Australian, Bedlington, Border, Cairn, Dandie Dinmont, Smooth and Wire Fox, Lakeland, Norfolk, Norwich, Scottish, Sealyham, Skye, Welsh and West Highland White Terriers as well as Dachshunds. The dogs need no prior training for this terrier sport. There is a qualifying test on the day of the event, so dog and handler learn the rules on the spot. These tests, or "digs," sometimes end with informal races in the late afternoon.

Here are some of the extracurricular obedience and racing activities that are not regulated by the AKC or UKC, but are generally run by clubs or a group of dog fanciers and are often open to all.

Canine Freestyle This activity is something new on the scene and is variously likened to dancing, dressage or ice skating. It is meant to show the athleticism of the dog, but also requires showmanship on the part of the dog's handler. If you and your dog like to ham it up for friends, you might want to look into freestyle.

Lure coursing lets sighthounds do what they do best—run!

Scent Hurdle Racing Scent hurdle racing is purely a fun activity sponsored by obedience clubs with members forming competing teams. The height of the hurdles is based on the size of the shortest dog on the team. On a signal, one team dog is released on each of two side-by-side courses and must clear every hurdle before picking up its own dumbbell from a platform and returning over the jumps to the handler. As each dog returns, the next on that team is sent. Of course, that is what the dogs are supposed to do. When the dogs improvise (going under or around the hurdles, stealing another dog's dumbbell, and so forth), it no doubt frustrates the handlers, but just adds to the fun for everyone else.

Flyball This type of racing is similar, but after negotiating the four hurdles, the dog comes to a flyball box, steps on a lever that releases a tennis ball into the air, catches the ball and returns over the hurdles to the starting point. This game also becomes extremely fun for spectators because the dogs sometimes cheat by catching a ball released by the dog in the next lane. Three titles can be earned—Flyball Dog (F.D.), Flyball Dog Excellent (F.D.X.) and Flyball Dog Champion (Fb.D.Ch.)—all awarded by the North American Flyball Association, Inc.

Dogsledding The name conjures up the Rocky Mountains or the frigid North, but you can find dogsled clubs in such unlikely spots as Maryland, North Carolina and Virginia! Dogsledding is primarily for the Nordic breeds such as the Alaskan Malamutes, Siberian Huskies and Samoyeds, but other breeds can try. There are some practical backyard applications to this sport, too. With parental supervision, almost any strong dog could pull a child's sled.

Coming over the A-frame on an agility course.

These are just some of the many recreational ways you can get to know and understand your multifaceted dog better and have fun doing it.

Your Dog
and your
Family

by Bardi McLennan

Adding a dog automatically increases your family by one, no matter whether you live alone in an apartment or are part of a mother, father and six kids household. The single-person family is fair game for numerous and varied canine misconceptions as to who is dog and who pays the bills, whereas a dog in a houseful of children will consider himself to be just one of the gang, littermates all. One dog and one child may give a dog reason to believe they are both kids or both dogs. Either interpretation requires parental supervision and sometimes speedy intervention.

As soon as one paw goes through the door into your home, Rufus (or Rufina) has to make many adjustments to become a part of your family. Your job is to make him fit in as painlessly as possible. An older dog may have some frame of reference from past experience, but to a 10-week-old puppy, everything is brand new: people, furniture, stairs, when and where people eat, sleep or watch TV, his own place and everyone else's space, smells, sounds, outdoors—everything!

Puppies, and newly acquired dogs of any age, do not need what we think of as "freedom." If you leave a new dog or puppy loose in the house, you will almost certainly return to chaotic destruction and the dog will forever after equate your homecoming with a time of punishment to be dreaded. It is unfair to give your dog what amounts to "freedom to get into trouble." Instead, confine him to a crate for brief periods of your absence (up to three or four hours) and, for the long haul, a workday for example, confine him to one untrashable area with his own toys, a bowl of water and a radio left on (low) in another room.

Lots of pets get along with each other just fine.

For the first few days, when not confined, put Rufus on a long leash tied to your wrist or waist. This umbilical cord method enables the dog to learn all about you from your body language and voice, and to learn by his own actions which things in the house are NO! and which ones are rewarded by "Good dog." House-training will be easier with the pup always by your side. Speaking of which, accidents do happen. That goal of "completely housetrained" takes up to a year, or the length of time it takes the pup to mature.

The All-Adult Family

Most dogs in an adults-only household today are likely to be latchkey pets, with no one home all day but the dog. When you return after a tough day on the job, the dog can and should be your relaxation therapy. But going home can instead be a daily frustration.

Separation anxiety is a very common problem for the dog in a working household. It may begin with whines and barks of loneliness, but it will soon escalate into a frenzied destruction derby. That is why it is so important to set aside the time to teach a dog to relax when left alone in his confined area and to understand that he can trust you to return.

Let the dog get used to your work schedule in easy stages. Confine him to one room and go in and out of that room over and over again. Be casual about it. No physical, voice or eye contact. When the pup no longer even notices your comings and goings, leave the house for varying lengths of time, returning to stay home for a few minutes and gradually increasing the time away. This training can take days, but the dog is learning that you haven't left him forever and that he can trust you.

Any time you leave the dog, but especially during this training period, be casual about your departure. No anxiety-building fond farewells. Just "Bye" and go! Remember the "Good dog" when you return to find everything more or less as you left it.

If things are a mess (or even a disaster) when you return, greet the dog, take him outside to eliminate, and then put him in his crate while you clean up. Rant and rave in the shower! *Do not* punish the dog. You were not there when it happened, and the rule is: Only punish as you catch the dog in the act of wrongdoing. Obviously, it makes sense to get your latchkey puppy when you'll have a week or two to spend on these training essentials.

Family weekend activities should include Rufus whenever possible. Depending on the pup's age, now is the time for a long walk in the park, playtime in the backyard, a hike in the woods. Socializing is as important as health care, good food and physical exercise, so visiting Aunt Emma or Uncle Harry and the next-door neighbor's dog or cat is essential to developing an out-going, friendly temperament in your pet.

If you are a single adult, socializing Rufus at home and away will prevent him from becoming overly protective of you (or just overly attached) and will also prevent such behavioral problems as dominance or fear of strangers.

Babies

Whether already here or on the way, babies figure larger than life in the eyes of a dog. If the dog is there first, let him in on all your baby preparations in the house. When baby arrives, let Rufus sniff any item of clothing that has been on the baby before Junior comes home. Then let Mom greet the dog first before introducing the new family member. Hold the baby down for the dog to see and sniff, but make sure some-one's holding the dog on lead in case of any sudden moves. Don't play keep-away or tease the dog with the baby, which only invites undesirable jump-ing up.

The dog and the baby are "family," and for starters can be treated almost as equals. Things rapidly change, however, espe-cially when baby takes to creeping around on all fours on the dog's turf or, better yet, has yummy pudding all over her face and hands! That's when a lot of things in the dog's and baby's lives become more separate than equal.

Dogs are perfect confidants.

Toddlers make terrible dog owners, but if you can't avoid the combination, use patient discipline (that is, positive teaching rather than punishment), and use time-outs before you run out of patience.

A dog and a baby (or toddler, or an assertive young child) should never be left alone together. Take the dog with you or confine him. With a baby or youngsters in the house, you'll have plenty of use for that wonderful canine safety device called a crate!

Young Children

Any dog in a house with kids will behave pretty much as the kids do, good or bad. But even good dogs and good children can get into trouble when play becomes rowdy and active.

Teach children how to play nicely with a puppy.

Legs bobbing up and down, shrill voices screeching, a ball hurtling overhead, all add up to exuberant frustration for a dog who's just trying to be part of the gang. In a pack of puppies, any legs or toys being chased would be caught by a set of teeth, and all the pups involved would understand that is how the game is played. Kids do not understand this, nor do parents tolerate it. Bring Rufus indoors before you have reason to regret it. This is time-out, not a punishment.

You can explain the situation to the children and tell them they must play quieter games until the puppy learns not to grab them with his mouth. Unfortunately, you can't explain it that easily to the dog. With adult supervision, they will learn how to play together.

Young children love to tease. Sticking their faces or wiggling their hands or fingers in the dog's face is teasing. To another person it might be just annoying, but it is threatening to a dog. There's another difference: We can make the child stop by an explanation, but the only way a dog can stop it is with a warning growl and then with teeth. Teasing is the major cause of children being bitten by their pets. Treat it seriously.

Older Children

The best age for a child to get a first dog is between the ages of 8 and 12. That's when kids are able to accept some real responsibility for their pet. Even so, take the child's vow of "I will never *ever* forget to feed (brush, walk, etc.) the dog" for what it's worth: a child's good intention at that moment. Most kids today have extra lessons, soccer practice, Little League, ballet, and so forth piled on top of school schedules. There will be many times when Mom will have to come to the dog's rescue. "I walked the dog for you so you can set the table for me" is one way to get around a missed appointment without laying on blame or guilt.

Kids in this age group make excellent obedience trainers because they are into the teaching/learning process themselves and they lack the self-consciousness of adults. Attending a dog show is something the whole family can enjoy, and watching Junior Showmanship may catch the eye of the kids. Older children can begin to get involved in many of the recreational activities that were reviewed in the previous chapter. Some of the agility obstacles, for example, can be set up in the backyard as a family project (with an adult making sure all the equipment is safe and secure for the dog).

Older kids are also beginning to look to the future, and may envision themselves as veterinarians or trainers or show dog handlers or writers of the next Lassie best-seller. Dogs are perfect confidants for these dreams. They won't tell a soul.

Other Pets

Introduce all pets tactfully. In a dog/cat situation, hold the dog, not the cat. Let two dogs meet on neutral turf—a stroll in the park or a walk down the street—with both on loose leads to permit all the normal canine ways of saying hello, including routine sniffing, circling, more sniffing, and so on. Small creatures such as hamsters, chinchillas or mice must be kept safe from their natural predators (dogs and cats).

Festive Family Occasions

Parties are great for people, but not necessarily for puppies. Until all the guests have arrived, put the dog in his crate or in a room where he won't be disturbed. A socialized dog can join the fun later as long as he's not underfoot, annoying guests or into the hors d'oeuvres.

There are a few dangers to consider, too. Doors opening and closing can allow a puppy to slip out unnoticed in the confusion, and you'll be organizing a search party instead of playing host or hostess. Party food and buffet service are not for dogs. Let Rufus party in his crate with a nice big dog biscuit.

At Christmas time, not only are tree decorations dangerous and breakable (and perhaps family heirlooms), but extreme caution should be taken with the lights, cords and outlets for the tree lights and any other festive lighting. Occasionally a dog lifts a leg, ignoring the fact that the tree is indoors. To avoid this, use a canine repellent, made for gardens, on the tree. Or keep him out of the tree room unless supervised. And whatever you do, *don't* invite trouble by hanging his toys on the tree!

Car Travel

Before you plan a vacation by car or RV with Rufus, be sure he enjoys car travel. Nothing spoils a holiday quicker than a carsick dog! Work within the dog's comfort level. Get in the car with the dog in his crate or attached to a canine car safety belt and just sit there until he relaxes. That's all. Next time, get in the car, turn on the engine and go nowhere. Just sit. When that is okay, turn on the engine and go around the block. Now you can go for a ride and include a stop where you get out, leaving the dog for a minute or two.

On a warm day, always park in the shade and leave windows open several inches. And return quickly. It only takes 10 minutes for a car to become an overheated steel death trap.

Motel or Pet Motel?

Not all motels or hotels accept pets, but you have a much better choice today than even a few years ago. To find a dog-friendly lodging, look at *On the Road Again With Man's Best Friend,* a series of directories that detail bed and breakfasts, inns, family resorts and other hotels/motels. Some places require a refundable deposit to cover any damage incurred by the dog. More B&Bs accept pets now, but some restrict the size.

If taking Rufus with you is not feasible, check out boarding kennels in your area. Your veterinarian may offer this service, or recommend a kennel or two he or she is familiar with. Go see the facilities for yourself, ask about exercise, diet, housing, and so on. Or, if you'd rather have Rufus stay home, look into bonded petsitters, many of whom will also bring in the mail and water your plants.

chapter 11

Your Dog
and your
Community

by Bardi McLennan

Step outside your home with your dog and you are no longer just family, you are both part of your community. This is when the phrase "responsible pet ownership" takes on serious implications. For starters, it means you pick up after your dog—not just occasionally, but every time your dog eliminates away from home. That means you have joined the Plastic Baggy Brigade! You always have plastic sandwich bags in your pocket and several in the car. It means you teach your kids how to use them, too. If you think this is "yucky," just imagine what

the person (a non-doggy person) who inadvertently steps in the mess thinks!

Your responsibility extends to your neighbors: To their ears (no annoying barking); to their property (their garbage, their lawn, their flower beds, their cat— especially their cat); to their kids (on bikes, at play); to their kids' toys and sports equipment.

There are numerous dog-related laws, ranging from simple dog licensing and leash laws to those holding you liable for any physical injury or property damage done by your dog. These laws are in place to protect everyone in the community, including you and your dog. There are town ordinances and state laws which are by no means the same in all towns or all states. Ignorance of the law won't get you off the hook. The time to find out what the laws are where you live is now.

Be sure your dog's license is current. This is not just a good local ordinance, it can make the difference between finding your lost dog or not. Many states now require proof of rabies vaccination and that the dog has been spayed or neutered before issuing a license. At the same time, keep up the dog's annual immunizations.

Dressing your dog up makes him appealing to strangers.

Never let your dog run loose in the neighborhood. This will not only keep you on the right side of the leash law, it's the outdoor version of the rule about not giving your dog "freedom to get into trouble."

Good Canine Citizen

Sometimes it's hard for a dog's owner to assess whether or not the dog is sufficiently socialized to be accepted by the community at large. Does Rufus or Rufina display good, controlled behavior in public? The AKC's Canine Good Citizen program is available through many dog organizations. If your dog passes the test, the title "CGC" is earned.

The overall purpose is to turn your dog into a good neighbor and to teach you about your responsibility to your community as a dog owner. Here are the ten things your dog must do willingly:

1. Accept a stranger stopping to chat with you.
2. Sit and be petted by a stranger.
3. Allow a stranger to handle him or her as a groomer or veterinarian would.
4. Walk nicely on a loose lead.
5. Walk calmly through a crowd.
6. Sit and down on command, then stay in a sit or down position while you walk away.
7. Come when called.
8. Casually greet another dog.
9. React confidently to distractions.
10. Accept being left alone with someone other than you and not become overly agitated or nervous.

Schools and Dogs

Schools are getting involved with pet ownership on an educational level. It has been proven that children who are kind to animals are humane in their attitude toward other people as adults.

A dog is a child's best friend, and so children are often primary pet owners, if not the primary caregivers. Unfortunately, they are also the ones most often bitten by dogs. This occurs due to a lack of understanding that pets, no matter how sweet, cuddly and loving, are still animals. Schools, along with parents, dog clubs, dog fanciers and the AKC, are working to change all that with video programs for children not only in grade school, but in the nursery school and pre-kindergarten age group. Teaching youngsters how to be responsible dog owners is important community work. When your dog has a CGC, volunteer to take part in an educational classroom event put on by your dog club.

Boy Scout Merit Badge

A Merit Badge for Dog Care can be earned by any Boy Scout ages 11 to 18. The requirements are not easy, but amount to a complete course in responsible dog care and general ownership. Here are just a few of the things a Scout must do to earn that badge:

Point out ten parts of the dog using the correct names.

Give a report (signed by parent or guardian) on your care of the dog (feeding, food used, housing, exercising, grooming and bathing), plus what has been done to keep the dog healthy.

Explain the right way to obedience train a dog, and demonstrate three comments.

Several of the requirements have to do with health care, including first aid, handling a hurt dog, and the dangers of home treatment for a serious ailment.

The final requirement is to know the local laws and ordinances involving dogs.

There are similar programs for Girl Scouts and 4-H members.

Local Clubs

Local dog clubs are no longer in existence just to put on a yearly dog show. Today, they are apt to be the hub of the community's involvement with pets. Dog clubs conduct educational forums with big-name speakers, stage demonstrations of canine talent in a busy mall and take dogs of various breeds to schools for classroom discussion.

The quickest way to feel accepted as a member in a club is to volunteer your services! Offer to help with something—anything—and watch your popularity (and your interest) grow.

Therapy Dogs

Once your dog has earned that essential CGC and reliably demonstrates a steady, calm temperament, you could look into what therapy dogs are doing in your area.

Therapy dogs go with their owners to visit patients at hospitals or nursing homes, generally remaining on leash but able to coax a pat from a stiffened hand, a smile from a blank face, a few words from sealed lips or a hug from someone in need of love.

Nursing homes cover a wide range of patient care. Some specialize in care of the elderly, some in the treatment of specific illnesses, some in physical therapy. Children's facilities also welcome visits from trained therapy dogs for boosting morale in their pediatric patients. Hospice care for the terminally ill and the at-home care of AIDS patients are other areas where this canine visiting is desperately needed. Therapy dog training comes first.

Your dog can make a differ-ence in lots of lives.

There is a lot more involved than just taking your nice friendly pooch to someone's bedside. Doing therapy dog work involves your own emotional stability as well as that of your dog. But once you have met all the requirements for this work, making the rounds once a week or once a month with your therapy dog is possibly the most rewarding of all community activities.

Disaster Aid

This community service is definitely not for everyone, partly because it is time-consuming. The initial training is rigorous, and there can be no let-up in the continuing workouts, because members are on call 24 hours a day to go wherever they are needed at a moment's notice. But if you think you would like to be able to assist in a disaster, look into search-and-rescue work. The network of search-and-rescue volunteers is worldwide, and all members of the American Rescue Dog Association (ARDA) who are qualified to do this work are volunteers who train and maintain their own dogs.

Physical Aid

Most people are familiar with Seeing Eye dogs, which serve as blind people's eyes, but not with all the other work that dogs are trained to do to assist the disabled. Dogs are also specially trained to pull wheelchairs, carry school books, pick up dropped objects, open and close doors. Some also are ears for the deaf. All these assistance-trained dogs, by the way, are allowed anywhere "No Pet" signs exist (as are therapy dogs when

Making the rounds with your therapy dog can be very rewarding.

properly identified). Getting started in any of this fascinating work requires a background in dog training and canine behavior, but there are also volunteer jobs ranging from answering the phone to cleaning out kennels to providing a foster home for a puppy. You have only to ask.

part four

Beyond the Basics

chapter 12

Recommended Reading

Books

ABOUT HEALTH CARE

Ackerman, Lowell. *Guide to Skin and Haircoat Problems in Dogs.* Loveland, Colo.: Alpine Publications, 1994.

Alderton, David. *The Dog Care Manual.* Hauppauge, N.Y.: Barron's Educational Series, Inc., 1986.

American Kennel Club. *American Kennel Club Dog Care and Training.* New York: Howell Book House, 1991.

Bamberger, Michelle, DVM. *Help! The Quick Guide to First Aid for Your Dog.* New York: Howell Book House, 1995.

Carlson, Delbert, DVM, and James Giffin, MD. *Dog Owner's Home Veterinary Handbook.* New York: Howell Book House, 1992.

DeBitetto, James, DVM, and Sarah Hodgson. *You & Your Puppy.* New York: Howell Book House, 1995.

Humphries, Jim, DVM. *Dr. Jim's Animal Clinic for Dogs.* New York: Howell Book House, 1994.

McGinnis, Terri. *The Well Dog Book.* New York: Random House, 1991.

Pitcairn, Richard and Susan. *Natural Health for Dogs.* Emmaus, Pa.: Rodale Press, 1982.

ABOUT DOG SHOWS

Hall, Lynn. *Dog Showing for Beginners.* New York: Howell Book House, 1994.

Nichols, Virginia Tuck. *How to Show Your Own Dog.* Neptune, N. J.: TFH, 1970.

Vanacore, Connie. *Dog Showing, An Owner's Guide.* New York: Howell Book House, 1990.

About Training

Ammen, Amy. *Training in No Time.* New York: Howell Book House, 1995.

Baer, Ted. *Communicating With Your Dog.* Hauppauge, N.Y.: Barron's Educational Series, Inc., 1989.

Benjamin, Carol Lea. *Dog Problems.* New York: Howell Book House, 1989.

Benjamin, Carol Lea. *Dog Training for Kids.* New York: Howell Book House, 1988.

Benjamin, Carol Lea. *Mother Knows Best.* New York: Howell Book House, 1985.

Benjamin, Carol Lea. *Surviving Your Dog's Adolescence.* New York: Howell Book House, 1993.

Bohnenkamp, Gwen. *Manners for the Modern Dog.* San Francisco: Perfect Paws, 1990.

Dibra, Bashkim. *Dog Training by Bash.* New York: Dell, 1992.

Dunbar, Ian, PhD, MRCVS. *Dr. Dunbar's Good Little Dog Book,* James & Kenneth Publishers, 2140 Shattuck Ave. #2406, Berkeley, Calif. 94704. (510) 658–8588. Order from the publisher.

Dunbar, Ian, PhD, MRCVS. *How to Teach a New Dog Old Tricks,* James & Kenneth Publishers. Order from the publisher; address above.

Dunbar, Ian, PhD, MRCVS, and Gwen Bohnenkamp. Booklets on *Preventing Aggression; Housetraining; Chewing; Digging; Barking; Socialization; Fearfulness; and Fighting,* James & Kenneth Publishers. Order from the publisher; address above.

Evans, Job Michael. *People, Pooches and Problems.* New York: Howell Book House, 1991.

Kilcommons, Brian and Sarah Wilson. *Good Owners, Great Dogs.* New York: Warner Books, 1992.

McMains, Joel M. *Dog Logic—Companion Obedience.* New York: Howell Book House, 1992.

Rutherford, Clarice and David H. Neil, MRCVS. *How to Raise a Puppy You Can Live With.* Loveland, Colo.: Alpine Publications, 1982.

Volhard, Jack and Melissa Bartlett. *What All Good Dogs Should Know: The Sensible Way to Train.* New York: Howell Book House, 1991.

About Breeding

Harris, Beth J. Finder. *Breeding a Litter, The Complete Book of Prenatal and Postnatal Care.* New York: Howell Book House, 1983.

Holst, Phyllis, DVM. *Canine Reproduction.* Loveland, Colo.: Alpine Publications, 1985.

Walkowicz, Chris and Bonnie Wilcox, DVM. *Successful Dog Breeding, The Complete Handbook of Canine Midwifery*. New York: Howell Book House, 1994.

ABOUT ACTIVITIES

American Rescue Dog Association. *Search and Rescue Dogs*. New York: Howell Book House, 1991.

Barwig, Susan and Stewart Hilliard. *Schutzhund*. New York: Howell Book House, 1991.

Beaman, Arthur S. *Lure Coursing*. New York: Howell Book House, 1994.

Daniels, Julie. *Enjoying Dog Agility—From Backyard to Competition*. New York: Doral Publishing, 1990.

Davis, Kathy Diamond. *Therapy Dogs*. New York: Howell Book House, 1992.

Gallup, Davis Anne. *Running With Man's Best Friend*. Loveland, Colo.: Alpine Publications, 1986.

Habgood, Dawn and Robert. *On the Road Again With Man's Best Friend*. New England, Mid-Atlantic, West Coast and Southeast editions. Selective guides to area bed and breakfasts, inns, hotels and resorts that welcome guests and their dogs. New York: Howell Book House, 1995.

Holland, Vergil S. *Herding Dogs*. New York: Howell Book House, 1994.

LaBelle, Charlene G. *Backpacking With Your Dog*. Loveland, Colo.: Alpine Publications, 1993.

Simmons-Moake, Jane. *Agility Training, The Fun Sport for All Dogs*. New York: Howell Book House, 1991.

Spencer, James B. *Hup! Training Flushing Spaniels the American Way*. New York: Howell Book House, 1992.

Spencer, James B. *Point! Training the All-Seasons Birddog*. New York: Howell Book House, 1995.

Tarrant, Bill. *Training the Hunting Retriever*. New York: Howell Book House, 1991.

Volhard, Jack and Wendy. *The Canine Good Citizen*. New York: Howell Book House, 1994.

General Titles

Haggerty, Captain Arthur J. *How to Get Your Pet Into Show Business*. New York: Howell Book House, 1994.

McLennan, Bardi. *Dogs and Kids, Parenting Tips*. New York: Howell Book House, 1993.

Moran, Patti J. *Pet Sitting for Profit, A Complete Manual for Professional Success*. New York: Howell Book House, 1992.

Scalisi, Danny and Libby Moses. *When Rover Just Won't Do, Over 2,000 Suggestions for Naming Your Dog.* New York: Howell Book House, 1993.

Sife, Wallace, PhD. *The Loss of a Pet.* New York: Howell Book House, 1993.

Wrede, Barbara J. *Civilizing Your Puppy.* Hauppauge, N.Y.: Barron's Educational Series, 1992.

Magazines

The AKC GAZETTE, The Official Journal for the Sport of Purebred Dogs. American Kennel Club, 51 Madison Ave., New York, NY.

Bloodlines Journal. United Kennel Club, 100 E. Kilgore Rd., Kalamazoo, MI.

Dog Fancy. Fancy Publications, 3 Burroughs, Irvine, CA 92718

Dog World. Maclean Hunter Publishing Corp., 29 N. Wacker Dr., Chicago, IL 60606.

Videos

"SIRIUS Puppy Training," by Ian Dunbar, PhD, MRCVS. James & Kenneth Publishers, 2140 Shattuck Ave. #2406, Berkeley, CA 94704. Order from the publisher.

"Training the Companion Dog," from Dr. Dunbar's British TV Series, James & Kenneth Publishers. (See address above).

The American Kennel Club produces videos on every breed of dog, as well as on hunting tests, field trials and other areas of interest to purebred dog owners. For more information, write to AKC/Video Fulfillment, 5580 Centerview Dr., Suite 200, Raleigh, NC 27606.

Resources

Breed Clubs

Every breed recognized by the American Kennel Club has a national (parent) club. National clubs are a great source of information on your breed. You can get the name of the secretary of the club by contacting:

The American Kennel Club
51 Madison Avenue
New York, NY 10010
(212) 696-8200

There are also numerous all-breed, individual breed, obedience, hunting and other special-interest dog clubs across the country. The American Kennel Club can provide you with a geographical list of clubs to find ones in your area. Contact them at the above address.

Registry Organizations

Registry organizations register purebred dogs. The American Kennel Club is the oldest and largest in this country, and currently recognizes over 130 breeds. The United Kennel Club registers some breeds the AKC doesn't (including the American Pit Bull Terrier and the Miniature Fox Terrier) as well as many of the same breeds. The others included here are for your reference; the AKC can provide you with a list of foreign registries.

American Kennel Club
51 Madison Avenue
New York, NY 10010

United Kennel Club (UKC)
100 E. Kilgore Road
Kalamazoo, MI 49001-5598

American Dog Breeders Assn.
P.O. Box 1771
Salt Lake City, UT 84110
(Registers American Pit Bull Terriers)

Canadian Kennel Club
89 Skyway Avenue
Etobicoke, Ontario
Canada M9W 6R4

National Stock Dog Registry
P.O. Box 402
Butler, IN 46721
(Registers working stock dogs)

Orthopedic Foundation for Animals (OFA)
2300 E. Nifong Blvd.
Columbia, MO 65201-3856
(Hip registry)

Activity Clubs

Write to these organizations for information on the activities they sponsor.

American Kennel Club
51 Madison Avenue
New York, NY 10010
(Conformation Shows, Obedience Trials, Field Trials and Hunting Tests, Agility, Canine Good

Citizen, Lure Coursing, Herding, Tracking,
Earthdog Tests, Coonhunting.)

United Kennel Club
100 E. Kilgore Road
Kalamazoo, MI 49001-5598
(Conformation Shows, Obedience Trials, Agility,
Hunting for Various Breeds, Terrier Trials and
more.)

North American Flyball Assn.
1342 Jeff St.
Ypsilanti, MI 48198

International Sled Dog Racing Assn.
P.O. Box 446
Norman, ID 83848-0446

North American Working Dog Assn., Inc.
Southeast Kreisgruppe
P.O. Box 833
Brunswick, GA 31521

Trainers

Association of Pet Dog Trainers
P.O. Box 385
Davis, CA 95617
(800) PET–DOGS

American Dog Trainers' Network
161 West 4th St.
New York, NY 10014
(212) 727–7257

**National Association of Dog Obedience
Instructors**
2286 East Steel Rd.
St. Johns, MI 48879

Associations

American Dog Owners Assn.
1654 Columbia Tpk.
Castleton, NY 12033
(Combats anti-dog legislation)

Delta Society
P.O. Box 1080
Renton, WA 98057-1080
(Promotes the human/animal bond through
pet-assisted therapy and other programs)

Dog Writers Assn. of America (DWAA)
Sally Cooper, Secy.
222 Woodchuck Ln.
Harwinton, CT 06791

National Assn. for Search and Rescue (NASAR)
P.O. Box 3709
Fairfax, VA 22038

Therapy Dogs International
6 Hilltop Road
Mendham, NJ 07945